Politics
in Sub-Saharan Africa

Roger Tangri

Reader in Public Administration
University of Malawi

JAMES CURREY
LONDON

HEINEMANN
PORTSMOUTH N.H.

James Currey Ltd
54b Thornhill Square, Islington, London N1 1BE, England

Heinemann Educational Books, Inc.
70 Court Street, Portsmouth, New Hampshire 03801, USA

British Library Cataloguing in Publication Data
Tangri, Roger
  Politics in Sub-Saharan Africa
  1. Africa, Sub-Saharan – Politics and government
  I. Title
  320.967   DT352.8
  ISBN 0-85255-300-5 (James Currey)

Library of Congress Cataloguing in Publication Data
Tangri, Roger
  Politics in Sub-Saharan Africa
  Bibliography:
  Includes index.
  1. Africa, Sub-Saharan – Politics and government – 1960-   I. Title.
  DT352.8.T35   1985   320.967   85-8520
  ISBN 0-435-08008-3 (Heinemann)

Chapter numbers hand drawn by Michael Harvey

Typeset in 10/11 pt Plantin
Printed in Great Britain

Politics in Sub-Saharan Africa

To Nick and Dan,
Kathi and Krissi

Contents

Preface

It was at Fourah Bay College, University of Sierra Leone in 1970 that I first started teaching a course on politics in Africa. In preparing that course, I was able to draw upon a variety of introductory texts and readers, and although the quality of much of this literature was subject to criticism, at least there was material available that was accessible to both students and teachers. Ten years later, this time at the University of Zambia, I once again began to teach a course on the politics of Africa. Preparing the course this time, however, proved to be a much more arduous affair. Not only had the study of African politics changed dramatically in the intervening decade but there were also hardly any works extant to introduce the student and teacher to the various themes and interpretations that had evolved during the 1970s. The principal purpose of the present work is to provide a text – although not a textbook – on African politics which may be of use to students and teachers in post-secondary institutions of learning as well as to the reader with a general interest in contemporary Africa.

To write about Africa is, of course, an enormous undertaking – sufficiently great that one can reasonably understand why so many have baulked at it. The extraordinary diversity of conditions and experiences makes generalization difficult. The present work seeks to circumvent this difficulty by concentrating, first, on Africa south of the Sahara. For various reasons – racial, geographic, and political – the Sahara constitutes a frontier. Egypt and North Africa have their main links with the Middle East and the Mediterranean and are treated here as external to sub-Saharan Africa. For similar reasons, certain other countries, including those in the Horn of Africa (such as Ethiopia, Somalia, and Sudan) are excluded, as are those such as Madagascar which are not a part of the African continent. A major omission is South Africa. Although intimately bound with other (and especially southern) African countries, South Africa's economic and social structure, history and politics has been very different. It is also not considered here because my concern is with independent African states in which the indigenous majority participates in government.

As a result of such exclusions, the range of variation in the countries dealt with in this book is not so great. Indeed the countries studied share many common features and broad uniformities. For instance, they all – excluding Liberia – came under European colonial rule in the latter part of the nineteenth century and attained independence in the post-Second World War period. During the colonial period they were 'articulated' with the world capitalist system, which generated over time a specific type of political economy leading, after independence, to these countries confronting similar economic and political problems. Although it has to be acknowledged that the area of Africa we examine contains within it a diversity of situations, nevertheless recurring patterns have appeared in the different states which make possible general treatment as well as some general statements.

To write a text on politics in Africa poses other considerable difficulties. The present work considers a number of topics covering key areas of political life in contemporary Africa. General agreement does not exist on what are the major political issues in Africa and there may well be subjects which many would regard as important but which have either been omitted here or treated all too briefly. No attempt has been made to be comprehensive in coverage of subject-matter, and I am conscious that some of the subjects considered have been as yet insufficiently studied. The study of peasant politics or scholarly work on various aspects of African international relations is still very much in its infancy. As an introductory text, however, this work attempts to provide a preliminary discussion of African politics based on the material available.

In treating these various topics, case-studies have been combined with more general discussion. The case-studies have been drawn from a select number of countries with which I have been familiar (such as Sierra Leone and Zambia), or which have been the focus of much scholarly work (Kenya, Nigeria and Tanzania). Such detailed studies may provide only a rough guide to political developments elsewhere on the continent but indications suggest that their findings are applicable to other African states. The present work also tends to concentrate largely on ex-Anglophone Africa. This is because in preparing this text there has been an almost total reliance on literature in the English language. Very little work has been published in English on, for example, the countries of French-speaking Africa, and although at times I have used works written in French (and German), I am assuming that both teachers and students will be mainly using literature in English.

But more important problems lie in the approaches to, and interpretation of, political data in Africa. Much controversy has been engendered through the advocation of rival approaches by 'bourgeois–liberal' and 'socialist–Marxist' scholars. My own view is that neither perspective is entirely right nor entirely wrong. Neither perspective possesses, moreover, a magic formula for understanding Africa's complex political situation, although at times certain perspectives have been closer to the political reality than others. The position I have adopted is a compound one: elements of it are to be found in the work and ideas of writers from both the rival camps. Adoption of a combined or eclectic position can yield various insights into political reality in contemporary Africa which may otherwise be overlooked or neglected in an analysis grounded in a particular perspective. Thus in the present work I have sought to combine the <u>class analysis of socialist writers with the patron–client and dependency approaches of liberal writers to</u> seek to comprehend diverse political phenomena in sub-Saharan Africa. The main intention of this work is to provide an introduction to the politics of contemporary Africa. If my intention has not been matched by what is contained here then I hope this book will stimulate others to try to satisfy what is at the moment a very important need.

I am deeply indebted to the Universities of Malawi, Sierra Leone and Zambia for providing me with the opportunity to teach and research various aspects of politics in Africa as well as for financial and other assistance to carry out my work. I have been ably assisted by the staff of these three university libraries as well as by the staff of the library of the Institut für Afrika-Kunde in Hamburg, West Germany, and wish to thank them for their unfailing kindness and co-operation.

I owe much to the comments and criticisms of others. Countless hours of discussion with students taught me much about politics in Africa. To students at the Universities of Malawi, Sierra Leone and Zambia I am deeply grateful. I am also very grateful to Judy Butterman, Christopher Clapham, Ken Good, Hugh Macmillan, Peter Meyns and Tim Shaw who have read parts of this book and saved me from many abuses of fact, logic and style. I owe special thanks to Bill Tordoff for going through the entire manuscript and whose detailed suggestions for improvement and general encouragement were particularly helpful. Any errors that remain are entirely my own responsibility.

Africa

SEYCHELLES

MOROCCO
Rabat
Algiers
Tunis
TUNISIA
Tripoli
ALGERIA
LIBYA
Cairo
EGYPT
El Aaiun
WESTERN SAHARA
MAURITANIA
Nouakchott
MALI
NIGER
CHAD
SUDAN
Khartoum
Dakar
SENEGAL
Banjul
GUINEA BISSAU
Bissau
Bamako
BURKINA-FASO
Niamey
Ouagadougou
N'djamena
DJIBOUTI
Djibouti
Addis Ababa
ETHIOPIA
GUINEA
Conakry
SIERRA LEONE
Freetown
NIGERIA
IVORY COAST
GHANA
TOGO
BENIN
Accra
Lagos
CENTRAL AFRICAN REPUBLIC
SOMALIA
Mogadishu
LIBERIA
Monrovia
Abidjan
CAMEROON
Yaounde
Bangui
EQUATORIAL GUINEA
Malabo
UGANDA
KENYA
SAO TOME & PRINCIPE
Libreville
CONGO
GABON
Kampala
Nairobi
RWANDA
Kigali
Brazzaville
Kinshasa
Bujumbura
BURUNDI
Cabinda
ZAIRE
TANZANIA
Dar es Salaam
COMORO ISLANDS
Luanda
MALAWI
Lilongwe
MADAGASCAR
Antananarivo
MAURITIUS
ANGOLA
ZAMBIA
Lusaka
MOZAMBIQUE
Harare
ZIMBABWE
Windhoek
NAMIBIA
BOTSWANA
Gaborone
Pretoria
Maputo
Mbabane
SWAZILAND
Maseru
LESOTHO
SOUTH AFRICA

CAPE VERDE ISLANDS

0 200 400 600 800 1000
kilometres

from *Africa Guide 1984*

Towards
Political Independence

By about 1900 the conquest of sub-Saharan Africa by Europeans was over. Only the Afro-American state of Liberia remained independent. Elsewhere the takeover by the European states – Britain, France, Belgium, Germany and Portugal – was complete. With the imposition of colonial rule, the political conditions for major economic and social change were also established; and fundamental changes were to be wrought in the material conditions of African societies. Roads, railways, modern medicine, technology, western education, Christianity and commerce now pushed into Africa. In turn, these changes were to create the conditions out of which the forces of anti-colonial politics would emerge, initially to challenge and later to overturn European colonial rule.

The colonial states were oriented towards achieving financial self-sufficiency; the colonial territories were to avoid being a burden on the metropolitan purse and the European taxpayer. They were consequently enjoined to pay their own way. As a result, some form of economic development had to be fostered, especially of a kind that would create taxable income for the colonial state. At the same time, Africa was looked upon within the overall metropolitan production system as a source of minerals and agricultural raw materials to service the needs of the metropoles. Thus the economies of the African colonies had to be reorganized primarily towards the export of minerals and/or primary agricultural commodities.

In certain parts of colonial Africa – such as the coastal territories of British and French West Africa and the British territory of Uganda in eastern Africa – the colonial state sought to establish its revenues and meet the needs of the metropolitan production system by building up peasant production of cash crops. Through the levying of customs duties on the imports of peasant producers as well as through the payment of direct taxes, they provided the revenues out of which colonial administration could be financed. Particularly in Uganda, Nigeria, the Gold Coast (Ghana) and Senegal, an astoundingly large percentage of the population was to become engaged in the agricultural production of cash crops – typically cash crops for export to Europe, such as groundnuts, cocoa, palm oil, rubber, cotton and coffee.

1

In other parts of Africa – known as white-settler Africa (Kenya, Northern and Southern Rhodesia [Zambia and Zimbabwe] for example) – only a tiny percentage of the African population was permitted to move into the category of independent producers of cash crops. In these colonial territories, a policy of limited settlement by Europeans was encouraged. Europeans, it was felt, would serve to employ and organize African labour on white-owned farms and plantations producing cash crops for export. Unlike West Africa, instead of being encouraged to grow cash crops on their own land, the Africans in much of eastern and southern Africa were 'encouraged' to earn the money they needed to pay their taxes by working as migrant labourers on European farms. And since white-settler Africa was also the area where mineral extractive industries were predominantly set up (producing tin, gold, diamonds, and other minerals), further numbers of migrant workers were to be induced to earn taxes by labouring in the mines. In the white-settler territories, therefore, there emerged, unlike elsewhere in Africa, a significant proportion of the African population in wage employment, although still not a very numerous one overall.

A variant of this second type of economic development stemmed from situations where countries were assigned a special economic role as labour reservoirs for producers in neighbouring territories. Thus countries which had few known natural resources or limited potential for peasant or European farming provided migrant workers for those that possessed such assets. Forced labour was practised in French West Africa from 1919 to 1946 with labourers being compelled to migrate from countries such as Upper Volta (Burkina Faso) to the farming areas of the Gold Coast and the Ivory Coast. In eastern Africa as well, many migrants from Nyasaland (Malawi), Mozambique, Bechuanaland (Botswana) and Basutoland (Lesotho) were obliged to seek work on the mines and farms of South Africa. Such labour-producing countries, whose prime economic function was that of a labour reserve, were to become highly dependent on income from labour migration. And among their African populations a class of worker-peasants was to be formed.

In some African countries, however, both peasant agriculture and settler farming developed. Nyasaland and Tanganyika (Tanzania) constitute examples. Moreover, in some West African countries such as the Gold Coast and Nigeria, where European settlement was extremely limited, urban African workforces emerged on account of the development of industries producing minerals for western markets. But typically one of the two main types of economic development was fostered in most of the colonial African territories.

Next to economic developments the introduction of western education was an important force of change in colonial Africa. In the British territories education was for long left primarily to missionary societies, whilst in French Africa consequent upon the secularist traditions of the

Third Republic education was the preserve of the government. But throughout Africa education became available on a gradually increasing scale. In the main, however, it was directed to a limited purpose. The missions desired teachers, catechists and lay preachers while the administration and foreign companies needed clerks and interpreters; few positions of greater eminence were to be open to Africans under the colonial system till after the Second World War. The mass of the pupils received only a minimal amount of educational exposure but a small minority were able to acquire more knowledge and skills.

The introduction of new, capitalist forms of economic development was accompanied by a new class formation in addition to – and to some extent replacing – the pre-capitalist forms of stratification in Africa. Over time, social stratification among Africans become more differentiated, with the spread of commodity production and education, and the growth of state machinery at both national and local levels. In brief, within the colonial economies there emerged a peasantry (itself stratified between the poor, the middle and the rich peasantry) along with a semi-proletarian rural mass and a small, nascent industrial working class. A rural and urban petty bourgeoisie also emerged (itself composed of different sections, such as traders and richer peasants) as well as an educated professional group composed of civil servants, teachers and lawyers. An extremely tiny indigenous or national bourgeoisie also became evident in a few countries, most notably in West Africa.

In the process of the consolidation of the colonial economy and society, there developed political contradictions between the Africans and the colonialists. As these contradictions were generated and became more intense there arose a resistance on the part of the people as a whole against the foreign occupier. An anti-colonial consciousness evolved which manifested itself in the demand for national political independence. The various African strata became united in their belief that the establishment of an independent national state was an essential prelude to their own subsequent economic and social advancement; the goal of African state sovereignty introduced an element of cohesion. The demand for national political independence, for the most part, was articulated by a deprived petty bourgeoisie and educated group, who were able to carry with them the masses of peasants and workers in their struggle against the colonial order. But divisions had also emerged within African society, which would become more pronounced in the post-colonial era. Class divisions, although muted in the colonial situation, would become politically prominent after the attainment of political independence.

It is important to realize, however, that the formation of classes was not a process implying the exclusion of non-class social identities. Other bases of solidarity – often stemming from the pre-colonial period – persisted and indeed developed thereafter. Identities such as those of kinship and ethnicity constituted key bases of solidarity. In the urban and rural areas of colonial Africa ethnic consciousness and identity co-existed therefore with evolving class consciousness. African political behaviour as a result was to be grounded in both class and non-class organizations and solidarities.

This chapter seeks to explore the political reactions of the various new classes that emerged in Africa during the colonial period, acknowledging at the same time that these political responses were also moulded at times by non-class social identities. In particular, I wish to relate the politics of the various classes to the subject of African nationalism or anti-colonialism. In dealing with the character of the African struggle against colonial rule, the discussion is focused on the role of particular classes as well as the organization, leadership and ideology of the nationalist movement and the nature of the transfer of power to Africans (entailing either peaceful political struggle or armed and violent upheaval). The study of anti-colonial and nationalist struggle is important as it has provided various legacies for post-colonial politics, some of which are indicated in the following discussion.

The politics of the urban African masses

The creation of an employed labour-force in Africa was essentially the product of European colonial rule. By the latter 1930s, within the new urban centres of tropical Africa, large numbers of workers were to be found engaged on public works programmes, in the extractive industries and on the railways and harbours, as well as being employed by the colonial administration and private employers in such positions as clerks, drivers or messengers. But wherever they worked, urban wage-earners were an exploited group and were apt to be subjected to much abuse and injustice in their work. Workers were badly paid, poorly fed, racially insulted, and forced to endure conditions at work which were often appalling. Conditions in mine compounds were especially notorious: those in Southern Rhodesia had dreadful health and labour-management records.[1] It was such working and living conditions that underlay workers' protest; African workers were driven to protest against low wages, hard work and harsh discipline. They gradually became conscious of their common interests as workers – rather than seeing themselves as persons from different tribal backgrounds – and made the first attempts to organize concerted resistance to improve their conditions.

Up to the Second World War, trade unions were not permitted to be formed by workers in most African countries. But although formal combination was prohibited, workers demonstrated an autonomous capacity for organization and action. The workers were far from being an inert and powerless group. In territory after territory, petitions were drawn up and presented by African workers demanding improved conditions. Writing about workers in the Southern Rhodesian mines, van Onselen states that between 1903 and 1912 'scarcely a year passed without some work stoppage or strike'.[2] And, similarly, elsewhere in Africa, and especially in eastern and southern Africa, workers' discontent was expressed in withdrawal of labour, with incidents of small-scale strikes, go-slows, and refusals to work becoming common.[3] At least as important as petitions and strike action were the informal ways of expressing grievances – loafing, desertion, slowdowns, and minor acts of sabotage – ways that 'formed the woof and warp of worker consciousness'.[4] Finally, economic organization in the form of trade unions, although not legally permitted, emerged to promote the interests of wage-earners. In spite of many of these unions being short-lived and intermittent, they concentrated wage-earning interests and challenged employers.[5]

Strike action, however, was especially significant. Although often on a small scale, and despite being illegal and ruthlessly suppressed, strikes were indicative of a growing solidarity among sections of the workforce. Collective action, resulting from the growing concentration of workers at work sites, was a common feature of the urban situation. The absence of formal labour organization in most places did not prevent workers from uniting in defence of their interests. In his reflections on this period, M. A. O. Imoudu, the militant Nigerian railway unionist, commented: 'We did not have an effective trade union organisation in the 1920s, but we had a lot of Nigerian workers who thought and acted like trade unionists.'[6] Through strike action workers were able to mobilize a wide range of workers, drawn from different ethnic backgrounds, and thus demonstrate an ability to act collectively on the basis of their shared interests as workers. Although most workers were short-term migrants – returning within a short period to their homes – in the different realm of the urban work-place they developed a consciousness of themselves as wage-earners and urban-dwellers as distinct from rural tribesmen. And over the years this consciousness was reflected in a willingness to take industrial action in the promotion of their interests.

A complex of socio-economic changes converged in the post-depression period and in the postwar years which resulted not only in the continued increase in the incidence of strike action and the occurrence of larger and better-organized strikes but also in the development of African labour organization. One important factor was the increasing numbers of Africans in non-agricultural, wage-earning employment in the urban areas. (By 1945, 61 per cent of all African workers in Kenya, for example, were in non-agricultural employment.) Their concentration in urban centres (at both work sites and residential areas) made possible large-scale strikes and labour organization.[7] Even more important was the gradual proletarianization of labour. Most workers remained migrant workers or seasonal workers working on short contracts. But in time, full-time workers emerged, who began to depend primarily, if not exclusively, on wages; wage-labour became the way of life for increasing numbers.[8] The development of proletarianized labour intensified demands for better living and working conditions. Migrant workers, who expected to be in their jobs for only a short period of time, were much more likely to accept their conditions; they perceived the situation to be only a temporary one from which they would soon escape. With more permanent labour, however, the need to improve conditions was essential, and full-time workers were more willing to engage in strike action to obtain the working conditions and wages they needed. Colonial Africa in the 1930s and 1940s began to witness major strikes – such as those on the Northern Rhodesian Copperbelt in 1935 and 1940, in Mombasa in 1939 and 1947, and among the French West African railway workers in 1947–8. Epstein remarks on the strike by the Northern Rhodesian copper miners: 'Although the labour force in the towns was still essentially migrant, the disturbances of 1940 showed plainly that the Africans were coming to regard themselves as industrial workers as well as members of different tribes.'[9]

The response of the colonial government was to set up new structures of communication to enable it to monitor evolving worker grievances and thereby stave off future conflicts. But these measures proved incapable of containing the recurring industrial unrest. Epstein has shown how the system of Tribal Representatives was instituted in the Northern Rhodesian copper mines to avoid the formation of trade unions and as a means for collective bargaining under the guidance of the colonial government's Labour Department. These representatives were rejected by the miners who began to initiate their own associations to promote their specific interests. In the copper-mine townships, Boss Boys' Committees emerged in 1942.

Boss boys – those in charge of a gang of labourers both surface and underground – were able to discuss with the Personnel Managers grievances or other matters relating to their particular employment. These committees were later superseded at all mines by Works' Committees. Mines clerks, who did not fall into the category of boss boys, felt that they had no real representation on the mines, and clerks' associations emerged from 1945 at a number of mines. Epstein argues that these various associations 'reflected the Africans' deep involvement in the industrial economy and an urban way of life'.[10] It appears therefore that the development of proletarianized labour was a precondition for the emergence of African collective labour organizations. African workers began to set up their own labour organizations before the colonial governments intervened to control them.

After much hesitation and concern about the appropriateness of the institution of trade unionism, the colonial authorities began, in the late 1940s, to encourage the creation of trade unions under guidance. It was hoped that unions would be successful in channelling industrial agitation into acceptable avenues as well as ensuring that the means of struggle for better wages and work conditions would be economic rather than political. African unionism had to evolve gradually and in such a way as to serve individual industries and remain non-political. Labour was organized into particular industrial sections or small-scale occupational bases – thus making solidarity with other workers more difficult – and workers were induced to pursue specifically economic aims rather than concerning themselves with political issues. As Bienefeld has observed in regard to the establishment of trade unions in Tanzania: 'The clear objective of this policy was to ensure that what trade union development did take place would be narrow, sectional, and relatively controllable.' The colonial state sought 'to control labour through the trade unions themselves'.[11]

The colonial authorities were largely successful in the promotion of industrial and non-political trade unions for Africans. Although industrial unrest, as reflected in strike action, continued to occur, it was invariably localized and confined to a particular industry. Workers' consciousness was focused on specific industries and failed to merge into a more expansive workers' solidarity. General strikes were very rare. Nigeria and Uganda in 1945, Sudan in 1947, and the Gold Coast in 1950 were some of the few examples. When workers from various industries did form a general workers' union, as was the case with the African Workers' Federation in Kenya in 1947, the potential power of such organizations was deemed too great to be permissible and they were explicitly opposed and undermined by colonial governments. Industrial action was also rarely directed into those political channels entailing anti-colonial agitation. The moment that this threatened to be the outcome, as in Kenya in 1950 when militant leaders of the East African Trades Union Congress became associated with the Kenya African Union, the colonial state quickly stepped in with repressive measures and encouraged rival trade-union organization. Given such external pressures as well as the emergence of moderate union leaderships, it is not surprising that when strikes did break out they were essentially expressions of discontent about the economic position of workers and represented attempts to force improvements in wages and labour conditions. Unions were successfully steered in a 'bread and butter' economist direction. The unions also eschewed association with nationalist organizations for another important reason; this was that workers saw in the trade unions a realistic hope for amelioration of certain economic grievances. Although other social groups in urban and rural society were to associate themselves with the goal of political independence as a necessary means of removing the obstacles to their mobility and economic advance (see below), many workers were able to achieve substantial reforms in the 1950s through the unions. The unions were therefore relatively apolitical in their orientation and were far from serving as overt instruments of attack on the colonial structure. Labour movements were only minimally involved with the nationalist movement.[12] Only very occasionally were there calls for political strikes and demonstrations by the unions, who further provided the nationalist parties with little in the way of financial or organizational assistance. This is not to deny the existence of some co-operation. But where it existed it was intermittent and was, as in Nigeria in the 1950s, often confined to elections. And where it threatened to evolve into a durable challenge to colonial rule – as was the case with the links between radical nationalists and labour leaders united in the Zikist movement in Nigeria in the late 1940s – the colonial authorities acted firmly and quickly to suppress such radical developments.[13] Moreover, there is some evidence that union members, although many were strong supporters of nationalist parties, saw the differentiation of party from union functions and personnel as best serving their interests. As was stated by mineworkers in Zambia after independence: 'We are all members of U.N.I.P. but don't bring politics into union matters.'[14]

Yet one must recognize that unions are not homogeneous organizations. They are often driven by differences in outlook between top leaders, branch leaders, and the rank and file. In the 1950s it is clear that the unions were little used for explicitly nationalist party objectives. But many individual unionists as well as the rank and file within the unions lent the nationalist politicians (amongst whom union members were also to be found) their staunch support. Of equal importance is the need to distinguish between the urban wage-earners and the trade unions which aspired to represent them. The unions often represented mainly the small number of white-collar and skilled workers who were typically the most proletarianized. The much larger number of manual, unskilled workers were less likely to be union members and less likely to channel their grievances through the organized union structure. Even if the unskilled workers were members (and probably about a third were on average), the leadership of the unions tended to be drawn from the white-collar and skilled workers. Thus, if the political militancy of the unions was limited, this should not be taken as an indicator of the political impact of the working class as a whole. In some African countries the unskilled workers, together with the non-wage labourers and the unemployed, played an important role in the nationalist upheaval.

The Kikuyu organization, *Anake wa 40*, or the 40 Age Group, played a central role in Nairobi African politics during the late 1940s and early 1950s. 'Its first members were the unemployed, petty traders, thieves, prostitutes and others of the lumpenproletariat of Nairobi.' Through the use of strikes, boycotts and assassinations and other forms of direct action, the leaders of the 40 Age Group directly confronted the colonial administration. 'They played,' writes Furedi, 'a pivotal role in the organising and financing of the "Mau Mau"[15] and also constituted an important source for the recruitment of Mau Mau fighters. The Kikuyu workers, in particular, had few or no land rights in the rural reserves and participated in Mau Mau partly in the hope of regaining access to their traditional land rights.[16] Moreover, workers were on an individual basis strong supporters of the nationalist movement partly because they hoped that nationalism (unlike the union) would bring about the betterment of their economic conditions as wage-earners. Although the unions had been able to obtain some improvements for the mass of workers, they were mainly influential in achieving gains for the more skilled and semi-skilled workers.

But in most African countries the evidence available suggests that the workers were not all that active politically. A united and politicized workers' movement hardly emerged and was effectively pre-empted by the colonial authorities. Even in the other segments of the urban social structure – the unemployed and those employed in petty trade and the informal sector – there appears to have been hardly any collective organization, consciousness and action on the part of this group in the political sphere. Perhaps this can be accounted for by the fact that the workers were only semi-proletarianized and could return to the rural areas. And perhaps also it would be in the rural areas that many of these workers would be politically involved by being linked with peasant protest when they returned to their rural homes.

The working class did not develop its own independent political party organizations during the colonial period. It followed the leadership of another class. As a result workers were not able to counteract the tendency of the petty bourgeoisie and educated elements which led the nationalist movement to present political independence as an end in itself. In ideological terms, the workers were to have little impact on the character of the nationalist movement. They were unable to arouse a more militant nationalism (than the one espoused by the petty bourgeoisie and the educated professional group) and they hardly articulated the demand that the nationalist movement be a socialist one. Even the 'lumpenproletariat' presented little threat to the colonial authorities. Urban populism, stemming from an alliance between these disparate elements of the labouring poor, would emerge only in the post-colonial era.

Rural African politics

In a number of colonial territories, mainly those in white-settler Africa, rebellions erupted shortly after European conquest. These rebellions were linked with developments in the rural areas. In Southern Rhodesia, the Ndebele and the Shona rose in 1896–7 in an attempt to drive out the white colonists who had taken their land. The Herero and then most of the Nama groups in German South-West Africa (Namibia) rose in armed revolt in 1904 against the German settlers who had occupied their land. The Maji Maji rebellion in German East Africa (Tanzania) in 1905 was also connected with white settlement but mainly with the weight of forced labour on state farms as well as the forcing of Africans to grow cotton on these farms. The 1915 rising in Nyasaland was connected with the brutal treatment of African tenant-labourers on white estates, and the alienation of land to Europeans. It was also a protest against forced African participation in the First World War as soldiers and as military porters, during which Africans in countries like Nyasaland, Northern Rhodesia and German East Africa witnessed intense suffering. John Chilembwe, the initiator of this rising, lodged a protest against the war which is worth quoting:

> Let the rich men, bankers, titled men, storekeepers, farmers and landlords go to war and get shot. Instead the poor Africans who have nothing to own in this present world, who in death leave only a line of widows and orphans in utter want and distress are invited to die for a cause which is not theirs.[17]

These large-scale rebellions, most of which were rebellions against colonial oppression and exploitation, were paralleled by innumerable small-scale protests. In many areas, religious leaders articulated rural discontent. Prophets in southern Nyasaland in 1907 and among the Gwembe Tonga of Northern Rhodesia in 1909 denounced the payment of taxes and called for the eviction of Europeans. Again in eastern and southern Africa other sorts of prophetic movements, particularly those associated with Watchtower (Jehovah's Witnesses), condemned the white man and his evil ways. In some areas, such as Mozambique, the people 'voted with their feet' and migrated in their thousands to neighbouring colonial territories to escape forced labour. Much of this protest, as well as the larger rebellions against colonial rule, was to be found in settler Africa where African rural grievances – emanating from the alienation of land; the herding of Africans into rural preserves bereft of good land and too small to cater for growing populations; the ill-treatment of workers on white estates; the force employed to recruit people as askaris and carriers – provided substantial cause to challenge white domination. In time other grievances arose which affected the interests of rural Africans in West Africa as well. Peasant producers specializing in export production were to voice incessant complaints about the prices offered for their crops; about not being able to transport their own produce but having to go through Asian, Lebanese or European contractors; and about government regulations and restrictions on the allocation of credit, and of extension services.[18]

The years between the world wars saw rural Africans expressing their grievances less often in violent form. To be sure violent protest was not absent. The Nandi protest of 1923 grew out of the accumulation of pressures on Kenyan Africans for land, labour and taxes. In 1929–30 there were extensive disturbances among the Igbo, Ibibio and Delta women of south-eastern Nigeria – 'The Women's War' – occasioned by rumours that women would soon be taxed. In 1931 a revolt erupted in northern Sierra Leone – the Haidara rebellion – resulting from the distress caused by falling producer prices during the economic depression. But all this violent protest – as in the case of earlier rebellions – was often grounded in the ethnic group and mounted by persons with tribal attachments. The rebellions were localized, defining themselves in regional or tribal terms. Moreover, these were generally small-scale revolts; large-scale collective violence was very rare (only in Cameroun and Kenya) and occurred mainly in the post-Second World War period.

The main example of the latter was the so-called Mau Mau insurrection in Kenya. The Kikuyu peoples had become increasingly militant in the post-Second World War years due to the severe socio-economic deprivations they were being subjected to. The increasing impoverishment of a great number of subsistence agriculturalists in the Kikuyu reserves as well as the deteriorating status of Kikuyu squatters on white farms led ultimately to revolt. In early 1950 an underground organization began to administer oaths to build up unity and commitment among the divided Kikuyu peoples. By the beginning of 1952 limited preparations commenced for armed resistance which, it was hoped, would create a crisis and force major concessions from the British colonial authorities. The original objective does not appear to have been a full-scale rebellion. But sporadic outbursts of terror and assassination, directed chiefly against Kikuyu who opposed the secret movement, led the authorities to detain the leaders and to force many of the movement's adherents into the forests where they were, over a period of years, to wage a bitter war against the white man. But like other manifestations of violent protest in rural Africa, the Mau Mau insurrection was severely put down, although unlike other such protest it did have some significance in the dismantling of the colonial order in Kenya.[19]

Constitutional means of achieving ends were more common. In the cash-crop producing areas within colonial territories, peasant societies had begun to emerge in the interwar period. Peasants – rural producers based on household labour who are integrated into the market economy through which they sell their product and upon which they rely to a major extent for provision of their own subsistence – are distinct from subsistence agriculturalists (who are not tied to the market) and full-scale farmers (who buy and sell their means of production). The peasants (who themselves can be stratified into poor, middle, and rich peasants) began to demonstrate an ability to organize themselves to advance their group interests. Iliffe writes: 'Since crop marketing is a peasant society's main connection with the larger polity and market of which it is a part, the marketing system often forms an important framework for political organization.'[20] Especially in cash-crop-producing areas in territories such as the Gold Coast, Nigeria, the Ivory Coast, Senegal, Uganda and Tanganyika, African peasants formed marketing co-operatives in order that the growers could strengthen their own position as against the buyers. In Tanganyika, where considerable discontent existed with the Asian-controlled monopoly buying system, co-operatives were started in the coffee-growing areas of Kilimanjaro and Bukoba in the late 1920s and 1930s which spread, particularly during the early 1950s, notably to the cotton-growing areas of Sukumaland. Here there was established, in 1955, the Victoria Federation of Co-operative Unions, the largest African-owned and operated co-operative organization on the continent. The Tanganyikan co-operatives were, at times, forums for the airing of political grievances of the peasantry. But as Iliffe notes: 'Like other peasants they only partly comprehended the source of their wrongs, attacking the local institutions which they could reach rather than the government or the world market which they either could not touch or did not understand.'[21]

Nevertheless, the peasants were beginning to display collective consciousness, organization and action. Examples of this were becoming evident. Discontent with the prices paid for produce sometimes led to a rural equivalent of industrial action, when the peasants sought to force buyers to pay them higher prices by withholding their crops. The outstanding examples in the interwar period were the three great cocoa hold-ups and trade boycotts in the Gold Coast in 1921, 1930–1 and 1937, which, although unsuccessful, demonstrated a willingness on the part of peasants to organize and act collectively against worsening terms of trade. Politically, however, they had limits. As Miles has shown, the hold-up movements 'never . . . assumed a political form, never moved beyond economic objectives, never demanded political changes as a means of achieving those objectives,.[22]

It was the bigger cash-crop producers – the richer peasants and farmers – who felt the full weight of colonial discriminatory policies and the vagaries of the market and became more politically conscious at an earlier date than did subsistence agriculturalists and poorer peasants. As a result the co-operatives that emerged were invariably formed by traders, richer peasants and 'kulak' farmers (those who, for instance, were able to employ labourers on their farms to expand their production). The co-operative institutions were not the product of a class struggle waged by the poorer peasants and subsistence agriculturalists. Rather, the co-operative movement provided an institutional base for the dominant class elements in the rural areas. Hyden has shown how the traders and successful farmers, sometimes in alliance with traditional leaders, spearheaded the co-operative movement in Tanganyika; similarly, Beckman has shown that in the Gold Coast the farmers' organizations set up in the interwar years and concerned with the marketing of cocoa were controlled by a stratum of big farmers and farmer-traders.[23] The mass of the peasants in contrast were relatively unorganized, and although many belonged to the co-operative movements these were primarily institutions in the interest of the richer peasants and farmers.

At times the co-operatives were given active support by the colonial government. Official support for co-operative marketing in the Gold Coast represented an attempt to create 'constitutional' outlets for African commercial aspirations and the desire to avoid confrontations such as the cocoa hold-up and trade boycott in 1937–8. Co-operative marketing in the early 1940s was seen as a way of preventing the cocoa-trade from becoming a platform for anti-colonial agitation. Similarly in Uganda the co-operative – the organizational expression of the 'kulak' farmers – was 'cultivated under the protective eye of the state and steered clear of political involvement'.[24] Especially during the 1940s the state sought to control co-operatives and direct them into politically safe channels. Just as in the case of trade unions in the urban areas, co-operative institutions in the rural areas were often controlled by the colonial state. Not only did they not generally become vehicles of anti-colonial agitation, but they also served as instruments dividing the African peoples in the rural countryside.

The mass of the peasants were little affected by marketing restrictions and had few deep-seated grievances. Lonsdale, in fact, writes of the 1920s in eastern Africa as a period when 'there were rarely acute peasant complaints to articulate'.[25] Only a very small fraction of persons in the rural areas had become involved in any form of social change which removed them decisively from pre-colonial patterns of life and work. The mass of peasants remained psychologically within the small-scale and self-contained subsistence economy. The personal needs of poor peasants were thus not altered and the colonial government did not experience mass pressures for greater services and opportunities. The needs of the peasants could be adequately satisfied by tribal government. Nor were there any serious external exactions imposed on the masses to provoke widespread rural disaffection. Production methods and land tenure, the most fundamental aspects of customary life, remained unaffected by direct governmental interference.

Be that as it may, a range of disillusionments was extant among the peasants, especially the peasants in eastern Africa whose grievances continued to revolve around issues relating to land, labour and tax; and those in French Africa where the corvée and other forced labour practices were widely extant. Although the degree of peasant misery was rarely acute, there did emerge protest and political action which was often expressed in non-secular guise. In eastern Africa, in particular, messianic religious movements arose which protested against the various injustices felt by peasants. Nevertheless, mass rural disaffection and agitation were not too evident in the interwar period.

But from the late 1930s and in the post-Second World War period the situation changed quite dramatically. The mass of the poorer peasants and subsistence producers began to become the focus of intensive efforts on the part of the colonial authorities to change methods of cultivation and animal husbandry to protect and safeguard natural resources. This was particularly the case throughout eastern Africa, where a series of rules and orders was passed imposing such measures as contour-ridging and cattle-destocking to regulate the pattern of farming. The rural masses became progressively disaffected by the coercive enforcement of such rules and restrictions and resented, as Cliffe argues, 'outside interference in the things closest to them, their land and its use, their cattle and their way of life'.[26] Popular resistance to agricultural regulations was at the heart of much of the rural discontent which was to be tapped by the nationalist politicians. In West Africa as well, though to a much smaller extent, considerable discontent ensued consequent upon government insistence that diseased cocoa trees be cut out under the swollen-shoot control programme.[27] In the Congo a policy of encouraging peasant agriculture by compulsory crop-production was introduced after the economic depression in the 1930s. In the post-war period, the so-called *paysannat indigène* scheme, whereby peasants were resettled to produce primary agricultural produce, also led to considerable discontent. Similarly in Mozambique forced cultivation of crops became a major source of discontent among the peasants, particularly in the late 1940s and early 1950s. Such was the level of exploitation, especially in the northern areas, that large numbers fled to neighbouring countries. Amongst the hundreds of thousands of migrants the nationalist organizations would find a fertile base for their anti-colonial agitation.

The conditions that spawned mass rural discontent were becoming widespread. But the emerging protest movements tended to be relatively localized and ethnically fragmented. Peasant protests were fairly restricted in scope, being limited in both number of participants and the extent of territory affected. By virtue of their isolation from one another (consequent upon such factors as their individual form of production), the peasantry was unable to transcend its ethnic barriers and to recognize by and for itself a broader social identity. The peasantry in colonial Africa – as against the bigger cash-crop producers – was not able to coalesce into larger formations let alone into a class with a clear class-consciousness. It remained for another group – the African petty bourgeoisie and educated elements – to provide the means for a wider understanding and to provide leadership for the rural masses.

Elite African pressure groups

In the cities and towns of colonial Africa, the first signs of modern political activity appeared in the associations organized and led by westernized, indigenous elites. These associations were controlled by a small entrepreneurial and professional group (such as lawyers) in West Africa and by clerks and teachers in eastern Africa. Class interests motivated much of this organizational activity. Those who had grasped the new opportunities in trade and education introduced by colonial rule had eventually found their opportunities for employment and advancement curtailed by the administrative, educational and commercial policies of the colonial state as well as by the actions and behaviour of foreign and settler capital. It was invariably such persons who formed associations concerned with their own particular class interests and identity. A variety of associations was established – traders' associations, civil servant groups, intellectual clubs – which were essentially elitist bodies mainly oriented towards a tiny privileged group concerned with self-improvement. Their influence, moreover, was effectively confined to a few municipal centres.

The first associations were started in West Africa, where a longer history of western education had produced a tiny educated minority. An early prominent organization, the National Congress of British West Africa, held its first meeting in 1920 at Accra, Gold Coast, and was attended mainly by professional men, especially lawyers and merchants. The elite members of the National Congress were chiefly concerned with their own exclusion from authority and opportunity. Other bodies of note included Herbert Macaulay's Nigerian National Democratic Party in Lagos. Like the members of the National Congress, politicans such as Macaulay were concerned with the lack of opportunities for African business enterprise, chafed at the virtual monopoly of trade enjoyed by European firms and demanded a greater say in government and thereby a larger influence over government policy. Like the National Congress, the Democratic Party did not seek to ally with the labouring poor in the urban centres although it did at times take up their problems. Similarly, the Youth Movements established from the late 1930s, although slightly more reformist groups, were organizations whose leadership was still in the hands of the African entrepreneurial and professional group and whose concerns revolved around the exclusion of their leaders from significant political influence as well as the problems confronting African businessmen. In the towns and countryside of eastern Africa as well, organizations were started by members of the African petty bourgeoisie (traders and richer peasants) and the educated professional group (clerks and teachers) all of whom were finding their path to further development blocked. In central Kenya in the late 1940s, for example, the association of the larger traders and producers was indistinguishable from political organizations such as the Kikuyu Central Association and the Kenya African Union. Although also concerned essentially with their class interests, these organizations, especially those in the rural areas, did occasionally address themselves to the plight of the rural masses. All of these associations, however, worked well within established institutions and did not dispute the legitimacy of the colonial order. They were far from agitating for the immediate end of colonial rule.[28]

Mention should also be made of the non-secular associations – in the form of independent African churches – which were much more concerned to provide some solution to problems afflicting urban workers and rural peasants. A number of such churches attempted, for example, to create independent schools to supply Africans with the knowledge and skills that mission churches and government organizations were failing to provide. But although some articulated discontent, their primary concern lay in non-political spheres. They had been established mainly because they desired church self-government and could, on the ecclesiastical plane, assert their independence of European authority. Such churches proliferated in white-settler Africa where highly authoritarian regimes blocked 'all other roads by which Africans might seek their emancipation'. Their importance 'as an outlet for social and political aspirations' declined in the post-1945 period when 'political parties, trade unions, and the like, have offered more promising techniques for solving the problems of African subordination and poverty'.[29]

It was only after the end of the Second World War that a new political era dawned and the tempo of African political activity greatly accelerated. The prewar associations were now superseded by or transformed into nationalist movements. Much more militant organizations, asserting the right of self-determination, began to be established by leaders drawn from less prestigious and less prosperous elements of the African population. This was especially the case in a number of West African countries where the politics of the 'notables' gave way to the politics of the petty bourgeoisie. In the Gold Coast, for instance, political organizations came to be led by persons drawn from a section of society hitherto unknown in national politics.[30] A group of men of petty-bourgeois origins, frustrated by the numerous barriers to their personal development imposed by the colonial administration, and with the gradualism of the older, more educated professional and business groups, started the Convention Peoples Party (CPP). In a radical departure from previous associations, the CPP put forward explicit demands for national political control and also sought to recruit support from all sections of the population. Similar developments began to occur in eastern Africa where African political organizations had, prior to the early 1950s, also been moderate bodies seeking reforms within the colonial system. But they too began to make increasingly strident demands for fundamental revisions of the political structures of colonialism. The leadership of the Tanganyika African National Union (TANU), for example, was under the influence of younger, more radical and educated people who began to articulate a more strongly nationalist position. They evoked considerable support from petty traders and small-scale farmers and all those who felt that within the colonial system there was little scope for their skills and ambitions. The CPP and TANU were nationalist movements, and it is to the character and nature of nationalism that we now turn.

Political nationalism

We have noted the emergence in the post-1945 period of militant, nationalist political movements. Just as nationalism began to reach its height, the colonial era was coming to an end in Africa. External pressures for change were exerted in the United Nations and in other parts of the 'Third World'. Within the European capitals, the political and economic costs of continued colonial rule were leading to a more favourable disposition towards African political independence. The principles of self-determination and self-government became acceptable in the 1950s, initially in Britain and then in France and Belgium. (Portugal, however, was only willing to decolonize in the 1970s, with important consequences, as we shall see, for the nationalist movements in the Portuguese-controlled colonial territories.) The dislodgement of the colonial administrative structure was doubtless hastened by the nationalist movements, but political independence was nonetheless attained relatively peacefully and non-violently in much of colonial Africa.

An examination of the anatomy of political nationalism in Africa is necessary. It is important to study the character of the political organization which achieved independence, and especially of the leadership which attained control of the state apparatus, in that they influenced, in decisive measure, the nature of the political system that evolved in post-colonial Africa.

The new leaders who assumed control of the political organizations after 1945 were drawn from sections of the African community different from those in the forefront during the interwar years. In this new phase political organization was undertaken by politicians drawn from, and allied with, the various sections of the petty bourgeoisie (traders, farmers, and richer peasants) as well as the educated professional group. Many among the petty bourgeoisie and educated elements were frustrated and disenchanted with the colonial government as well as with their African predecessors. Traders were subordinate to settler commercial capital and demanded an end to state-protected monopoly privileges; civil servants found themselves at the bottom of a racially structured government service and demanded an end to racial discrimination in pay and conditions of service; and 'kulak' farmers were resentful of state marketing boards and their buying monopoly. They believed that their grievances and deprivations could only be resolved through the attainment of political power, through which lay their way to prosperity. 'Seek ye first the political kingdom and all things shall be added unto it' was Kwame Nkrumah's maxim in the Gold Coast. Not only were the new politicians more militant in their demands – 'Self-Government Now!' was what the CPP called for at its inception in 1949 – but the leaders were also full-time activists. No longer was political activity the avocational interest of men whose major energies were absorbed elsewhere. The leadership was also determined to spread the appeal of their organizations to the masses and to lend their demands the force of mass support. The post-Second World War period was to see the rise of mass-based political nationalism under the direction of the petty bourgeoisie and educated elements.

The growth of nationalism was deeply rooted in the anti-colonial grievances of the rural and urban masses. National political leaders did not have to mobilize an apathetic peasantry and urban labour force. The strength of mass protest contributed much to the ultimate success of the independence movements. The nationalist organizations which eventually emerged throughout Africa were in essence an orchestration of diverse mass protests. The nationalist leaders galvanized a miscellany of complaints amongs the rural and urban poor into a focused opposition to the colonial regime. A variety of grievances was tapped by politicians: workers' unrest; complaints against government restrictions on African small-scale businessmen and co-operatives; protests against agricultural prices in cash-crop-producing regions and against the high price of imported goods in urban centres; anti-poll tax agitation in French Africa and land and labour agitation in much of British Africa; disaffection arising from legislation governing agricultural practices including the cutting out of swollen-shoot disease in cocoa trees in West Africa; and, of course, the general revulsion against the white man's racist behaviour and racial discrimination. In so capitalizing on a medley of protests, the leaders harnessed these diverse local frictions to the wider cause of anti-colonialism; the grievances of the masses would be righted once political independence had been achieved. The nationalist politicians were thereby able to legitimize both the demand for independence and their own position as leaders for independence.

The nationalist movement that emerged was thus an interlinked set of a variety of local protests, united loosely in a coalition aiming for autonomy. Nationalism in Africa did not demonstrate so much a surge of national consciousness as an ability by political leaders to unite a medley of protests for the purpose of achieving independence. And the factor that bound the diverse elements together was the common feeling of anti-colonialism. Their point of unity was their opposition to the colonial order.

The way the felt grievances of the masses were translated into anti-colonial sentiment differed from place to place. In the rural areas it would appear that the rural elites (or the rural-based petty bourgeoisie) were the key links between villagers and the town-based nationalist leaders. The intermediaries at the grass-roots were invariably traders, teachers, government clerks, mission employees or catechists, police officers or medical aides – 'men who had broken the bonds of rural life through education, experience, travel, study and employment'.[31] The role of traders in rural leadership has been noted widely. In western Kenya, for instance, Oginga Odinga's Luo Thrift and Trading Corporation was a key body in co-ordinating and articulating popular discontent. The traders themselves were often disenchanted with central government policies and were vitally concerned with altering these policies.[32] They were 'local men with central interests'.[33] Their political aims coincided with those of the nationalist leadership; both desired the replacement of central government by an African one which, they anticipated, would be more responsive to their needs.

In the rural areas as well, religious movements, farmers' organizations and co-operatives also provided the basis for communication networks; their organizers established links that offered the nationalist leaders access to the countryside. For example, in the Ivory Coast the Syndicat Agricole Africain, which was set up by Félix Houphouet-Boigny in 1944 as an organization representing the claims of African cash-crop farmers for equal treatment with European planters, played an important role in the creation of the Parti Démocratique de la Côte d'Ivoire (PDCI). Although in many parts of colonial Africa there was increasing alienation of the peasants from the chiefs, in a number of countries (Sierra Leone, Senegal, Northern Nigeria and Basutoland are leading examples), it was the chiefs who provided such links. In these countries the chiefs had not been used by the colonial authority to oppress the rural populace and had preserved their local leadership positions. Given also the fact that the nationalist politicians had close kinship ties with the traditional rulers and were drawn from chiefly families, the chiefs were able to serve as important intermediaries in the recruitment of support for, for example, the Sierra Leone Peoples Party (SLPP). Similarly in Senegal the Bloc Democratique Senegalais (BDS) organized its strength in close collaboration with the traditional rulers who were principally Muslim religious leaders. Léopold Senghor, the BDS leader, is reported to have stated: 'It was the Imams in the mosques who made our triumph.'[34]

The urban centres provided different avenues for interaction between the elite and the town-dwellers. In the Zambian Copperbelt 'home-boy' groups constituted the basic cells which were transformed into the United National Independence Party (UNIP), while in Treichville, a borough of Abidjan, the capital of the Ivory Coast, PDCI organizers 'seized upon tribal associations as the nuclei for the organization of party committees'.[35] On the other hand, the CPP built its organization in the urban areas very largely on the growing number of elementary school-leavers, petty-traders, small-scale contractors and businessmen – persons for whom urbanization had brought little but increasing contact with the crippling restrictions and disabilities of colonial rule. These were persons who were virtually unemployable in white-collar jobs. As small businessmen they could not compete with the European trading firms and the Levantine entrepreneurs and furthermore faced restrictions in securing licences and credit.

One should not exaggerate the extent of support that nationalist movements attained. In most African countries the popular base of nationalist movements was fairly narrow; only a few experienced the creation of truly mass parties. Especially in West Africa, the political organizations that achieved independence did not have to maximize their support on a large scale; they would be successful in their drive for independent statehood provided they could demonstrate a reasonable degree of support. In the 1952 elections in the Ivory Coast, the PDCI polled only about 33 per cent of those eligible to vote; in the Gold Coast in 1951, the CPP gained the voting support of about 30 per cent of voters;[36] and in Nigeria in the 1950s the need to contract alliances with organizations such as the unions was not considered politically essential. One plausible explanation for this would be that rapid decolonization, especially in West Africa, made mass nationalism unnecessary for the attainment of political independence. In most of Africa during the late 1950s and early 1960s, the colonial power quickly came to terms with the nationalist leadership regarding the transfer of power. As indicated below, this 'coming to terms' was important for the colonial power in that it resulted in a nationalist leadership willing to maintain the economic structures of the colonial economy. Rapid decolonization militated against the emergence of a nationalist leadership which would be more radical in orientation as well as one which would create organizations more national, coherent and ideological in character – as was to be the case, for example, in the Portuguese-controlled territories.

Furthermore, one should also not exaggerate the extent of unity in the nationalist struggle. It was clearly only in a minority of countries that one party monopolized the nationalist movement. Only a handful of countries, particularly those in eastern Africa, such as Nyasaland and Tanganyika, were able to unite the diverse local protests and social groups within the framework of a single nation-wide organization. In much of colonial Africa, although one party was dominant, other parties – some of considerable weight – existed as well. Most organizations were confined to particular regions and areas and it was in these only that they could maximize their support from rural and urban groups. The cases of Nigeria – with its three parties grounded in three distinctive regions – as well as the Congo and Uganda are only the most dramatic witness to the absence of a concerted and united move towards independence. This failure to construct a single and united independence movement stemmed from various factors, not least of which (as we shall see in the following chapter) were the divisions within the petty bourgeoisie and educated professional group which militated against it emerging as an integrated group.[37] Where the political leaders were divided into rival parties, in order to win support in a situation of political competition they appealed to ethnic and regional sentiments. The reason why so many African leaders were to feel a major need to create one-party states after independence derived, in part, from the structural problems of integration during the anti-colonial struggle.

Yet in whatever way they were linked together, it was a truism that in each political organization there were leaders and followers. There were therefore class differences even where the political leadership was drawn from fairly humble backgrounds. The nationalist movements, however, with their anti-colonial slogans, were able to give political expression and unity to the various African classes: to unite the petty bourgeoisie and the intellectuals with the peasants and workers. The way the political links were developed permitted class differences between the leadership and the masses to be transcended. Mobilization of support for the anti-colonial organizations was generally characterized by vertical recruitment. Political recruitment in both the rural and urban areas occurred along vertical lines with political leaders appealing for support for their organizations from those individuals and group members with whom they had ethnic and regional affiliations. This overall form of recruitment was to forge structures for the development of a clientelist form of politics and for the exercise of patronage. The patronage functions of vertical networks was further accentuated by the promises of material benefits made by political leaders in the process of campaigning for support.[38] Patron–client networks, a key form of political interaction and organization in post-colonial Africa, had their origins in the period of anti-colonial struggle.

The nationalist leaders, especially in West Africa, were a different genre of politicians from those that had organized the prewar elitist associations. Whereas their predecessors had consisted of professionals and prominent businessmen, the new politicians were young educated men of little to moderate means and included petty traders and contractors, clerical functionaries and teachers. Very few approached the financial and educational status of the previous propertied politicians. Many of these new leaders were, writes Wolpe, '"men on the make", individuals hopeful of converting newly obtained political position into social and economic gain'.[39] Their possessive individualism was born of widespread material deprivation. Julius Nyerere has written that, in Tanganyika.

many leaders of the independence struggle . . . were not against capitalism; they simply wanted its fruits, and saw independence as the means to that end. Indeed, many of the most active fighters in the independence movement were motivated – consciously or unconsciously – by the belief that only with independence could they attain that ideal of individual wealth which their education or their experience in the modern sector had established as a worthwhile goal.[40]

Similarly, Kwame Nkrumah was to write ten years after Ghana's independence:

The circumstances under which the CPP was formed resulted in its being a compromise organisation composed of some genuine revolutionaries but containing many of those who are interested in independence only so as to better themselves and to take the place of the previous colonial traders and businessmen.[41]

Because so many nationalist leaders were motivated by a personal desire for the fruits of capitalism, and because so few of them could have attained these fruits through their occupations (as small-scale traders, clerks and primary-school teachers) they were, unlike the earlier politicians from more prestigious and prosperous backgrounds, extremely dependent on their political offices 'for chop'. Their political activity during the nationalist struggle was therefore not entirely selfless. With independence their office-holding would facilitate the attainment of that 'ideal of individual wealth'.[42] The disinherited of the colonial era would become the privileged of the independence era.

The content and strategy of the nationalist movement were influenced, although not necessarily consciously, by the class background of its leaders and the ideology to which they subscribed. The leaders invariably endorsed elements of bourgeois ideology, such as the sacredness of private property and the legitimacy of private, capitalist enterprise. Moreover, although the needs of the African masses as a whole were often at the centre of their demands, the leadership did formulate policy which was in accord with its own particular interests. There was, for instance, considerable emphasis placed on the needs of the more 'privileged' elements of the African population – cash-crop farmers, traders, the better educated. These needs were concerned invariably with the barriers to accumulation of capital on the part of African entrepreneurs and what needed to be done to build up an indigenous entrepreneurial class. To be sure nationalist leaders emphasized that with independence the population as a whole would benefit. Control of government would bring with it control of government funds which would be allocated to social welfare measures in the interest of the African masses as a whole. But at the same time it was clear that independence would not bring with it any major economic transformation of the way the colonial economy was organized. However, certain economic disparities of the colonial era would be rectified and remedied. These would be for the benefit of the African masses as well as, of course, for the African ruling group. But the essential features of the colonial economic system – entailing capitalist production relations – would be preserved and perpetuated.

Yet this was not all that surprising. The imperialist powers had accepted the principle of self-determination and independence for their colonies but had been concerned to retain their economic interests in these territories. This entailed the encouragement of reliable persons as nationalist leaders, who would safeguard the existing conditions of capital accumulation and not be prone to undertake revolutionary action. The colonial governments lent their full weight to the building up of a nationalist leadership which would be 'responsible' and 'moderate'.[43] They were quick to undermine the radical elements within the African nationalist leadership and worked assiduously to cultivate one more responsive to their (especially economic) needs. Numerous examples could be given, but a particularly graphic one occurred in Cameroun during the 1950s when the French did their utmost to uproot and destroy the Union des Populations du Cameroun (UPC), a radical nationalist movement considered subversive of the existing economic and social order. After the banning of the UPC in 1955, the French progressively devolved political power to the moderate and conservative forces in the territory.[44]

The transition to political independence in the majority of African states during the late 1950s and early 1960s was a peaceful process. African nationalists did not have to carry out a protracted, armed struggle to win independence; the transfer of power was achieved as a result of peaceful political struggle and negotiations. As a consequence there was no dramatic break with the colonial power at the time of independence. With the exception of the savage wrecking operation carried out by the French in Guinea in 1958, the departing colonial power did not uproot its capital or personnel. Thus a vacuum within the social order did not ensue. Nor, in these circumstances, did a revolutionary consciousness emerge, as was to be the case with those ex-Portuguese states which arose out of a process of armed struggle in the 1970s. To be sure some countries (such as Kenya and Cameroun in the 1950s and Rhodesia in the 1970s) did experience some degree of armed struggle, but the armed forces did not achieve the military defeat of the colonial powers; independence was achieved through negotiation. This was not the case in the Portuguese colonies of Angola, Guinea-Bissau and Mozambique, where violence led to discontinuities in the social order following the withdrawal – through military reversals – of the colonial rulers.

In these territories, consequent upon resolute Portuguese opposition to any kind of independence for its colonies, African nationalists had to take up arms and wage long insurgencies for independence. These were people's wars whereby large segments of the African population were mobilized in the struggle for liberation. These liberation movements, coming through the fire of popular warfare against reactionary Portuguese colonialism, achieved a more revolutionary nationalism. In the liberation struggle various political developments occurred which forged a close link between the leadership and the mass of the people which served, according to Saul, not only 'to combat any temptation towards entrepreneurial aggrandizement on the part of the leadership' but also to build up popular consciousness and mass involvement.[45] Moreover, the deep involvement of the masses was to lead the liberation movements to advocate that a colonial struggle be accompanied by a restructuring of society along socialist lines. Along with revolt they worked for a socialist revolution.

In a somewhat similar manner, the South-West Africa People's Organization (SWAPO) in Namibia began during the 1970s to stress the class character of its struggle. It began to reject the notion that the struggle was simply an anti-colonial one and emphasize that it was a struggle in the interests of the masses against imperialism. The issue that popular armed struggle had thrown up was the kind of independence that would be attained. Would it be, as in the anti-colonial struggles earlier in colonial Africa, an independence that would merely lead to the white man being replaced by the African petty bourgeoisie? Or was the struggle much more in the interests of the African masses – the peasants and workers – where independence would be a step in the direction of constructing a socialist society? Nyerere has written: 'We campaigned against colonialism, against foreign domination. We did not campaign against capitalism or for socialism.' There was, as he emphasized, lack of ideological content during the independence struggle.[46] In the struggles of the 1970s, however, African political movements such as those in the Portuguese African colonies (and, although to a much lesser extent, Namibia) defined their national liberation struggles as an alliance of certain classes whose ultimate goal was a socialist society. For them liberation should lead beyond the defeat of colonialism to the overcoming of neo-colonialism.[47] Samora Machel has written:

> We often say that our great victory in the course of our struggle has been the fact that we were able to transform the armed struggle for national liberation into a revolution. In other words, our final aim is not to hoist a flag that is different from the Portuguese one, or to hold general elections – more or less honest – in which blacks instead of whites are elected, or to have a black President instead of a white governor . . . We affirm that our aim is to win total independence, to establish people's power, to build a New Society without exploitation for the benefit of all those who consider themselves Mozambican.[48]

As we shall see in subsequent chapters, the consequences of popular armed struggle on the post-colonial economic and political systems have been somewhat different from those states where the anti-colonial struggle was relatively peaceful and organized by a more moderate petty-bourgeois leadership.

NOTES

1   See Charles van Onselen, *Chibaro: African Mine Labour in Southern Rhodesia 1900-1933* (London, 1976) for graphic descriptions of such working and living conditions.
2   ibid., p. 22.
3   See, for example, the studies in Richard Sandbrook and Robin Cohen (eds.), *The Development of an African Working Class: Studies in Class Formation and Action* (London, 1975); Peter C. W. Gutkind, Robin Cohen and Jean Copans (eds.), *African Labour History* (Beverly Hills, 1978); and I. R. Phimister and C. van Onselen, *Studies in the History of African Mine Labour in Colonial Zimbabwe* (Gwelo, 1978).
4   van Onselen, op. cit., p. 227. See also Robin Cohen, 'Resistance and Hidden Forms of Consciousness Amongst African Workers', *Review of African Political Economy*, No. 19 (1980), pp. 8-22.
5   See Arnold Hughes and Robin Cohen, 'An Emerging Nigerian Working Class: The Lagos Experience 1897-1939', in Gutkind *et. al.*, op. cit., pp. 36-8.
6   Cited in Peter C. W. Gutkind, *The Emergent African Urban Proletariat* (Montreal, 1974), p. 7.
7   See, for example, Sharon Stichter, *Migrant Labour in Kenya; Capitalism and African Response, 1895-1975* London, 1982), pp. 110-112.
8   See, for example, Sharon Stichter, 'The Formation of a Working Class in Kenya', in Sandbrook and Cohen, op. cit., pp. 35-6. See also Godfrey Wilson, *An Essay on the Economics of Detribalisation in Northern Rhodesia* (Livingstone, 1941), Part I, p. 46.
9   A. L. Epstein, *Politics in an Urban African Community* (Manchester, 1958), p. 81.
10 ibid., pp. 82-3.
11 M. A. Bienefeld, 'Trade Unions, the Labour Process, and the Tanzanian State', *Journal of Modern African Studies*, 17, 4 (1979), pp. 561, 562.
12 See Elliot J. Berg and Jeffrey Butler, 'Trade Unions', in James S. Coleman and Carl G. Rosberg Jr., (eds.) *Political Parties and National Integration in Tropical Africa* (Berkeley, 1966), pp. 340-81.
13 Robin Cohen, *Labour and Politics in Nigeria 1945-71* (London, 1974), pp. 169-71.
14 Quoted in Robert H. Bates, *Unions, Parties and Political Development. A*

Study of Mineworkers in Zambia (New Haven, 1971), Chap. 7.

15 Frank Furedi, 'The African Crowd in Nairobi: Popular Movements and Elite Politics', *Journal of African History*, 14, 2 (1973), pp. 282, 287.

16 Sharon Stichter, 'Workers, Trade Unions, and the Mau Mau Rebellion', *Canadian Journal of African Studies*, 9, 2 (1975), pp. 266–9.

17 Quoted in George Shepperson and Thomas Price, *Independent African. John Chilembwe and the Origins, Setting and Significance of the Nyasaland Native Rising of 1915* (Edinburgh, 1958), pp. 234–5.

18 For a summary of the literature on rural political protest in colonial Africa, see Robert H. Bates, *Essays on the Political Economy of Rural Africa* (Cambridge, 1983), Chap. 4.

19 For a recent overview of the Mau Mau insurrection see John Newsinger, 'Revolt and Repression in Kenya. The "Mau Mau" Rebellion, 1952–1960', *Science and Society,* XLV, 2 (1981), p. 159–85.

20 John Iliffe, *A Modern History of Tanganyika* (Cambridge, 1979), p. 277.

21 ibid., p. 281.

22 John Miles, 'Rural Protest in the Gold Coast: The Cocoa Hold-Ups, 1908–1938', in Clive Dewey and A. G. Hopkins (eds.), *The Imperial Impact: Studies in the Economic History of Africa and India* (London, 1978), p. 168.

23 Goran Hyden (ed.), *Co-operatives in Tanzania. Problems of Organization Building* (Dar es Salaam, 1976); and Bjorn Beckman, *Organising the Farmers. Cocoa Politics and National Development in Ghana* (Uppsala, 1976).

24 Mahmood Mamdani *Politics and Class Formation in Uganda* (London, 1976), p. 197.

25 John Lonsdale, 'Some Origins of Nationalism in East Africa', *Journal of African History*, 9, 1, (1968), p. 138.

26 For eastern Africa there is a considerable literature on this subject but see, for instance, Lionel, R. Cliffe, 'Nationalism and the Reaction to Enforced Agricultural Change in Tanganyika during the Colonial Period', *Taamuli*, 1,1 (1970), pp. 3–15. The quotation is from p. 13.

27 For examples of mass rural discontent in West Africa, see Dennis Austin, *Politics in Ghana, 1946–1960* (London, 1964), pp. 59ff, 159ff; and Christopher Beer, *The Politics of Peasant Groups in Western Nigeria* (Ibadan, 1976), Chap. 3.

28 See, for instance, John Iliffe, 'The Age of Improvement and Differentiation (1907–45)' in I. N. Kimambo and A. J. Temu (eds.), *A History of Tanzania* (Nairobi, 1969), pp. 122–60; and Roger Tangri, 'Colonial and Settler Pressures and the African Move to the Politics of Representation and Union in Nyasaland', *Journal of African History*, 13, 2 (1971), pp. 251–304.

29 Thomas Hodgkin, *Nationalism in Colonial Africa* (London, 1956), pp. 104–6.

30 Richard Rathbone, 'Businessmen in Politics: Party Struggle in Ghana, 1949–57', *Journal of Development Studies*, 9, 3 (1973) pp. 395–7.

31 G. Andrew Maguire, *Toward 'Uhuru' in Tanzania. The Politics of Participation* (Cambridge, 1969), pp. 217–18.

32 Oginga Odinga, *Not Yet Uhuru* (London, 1967), p. 94.

33 Lonsdale, op. cit., p. 146.

34 Cited in William J. Foltz, 'Senegal', in Coleman and Rosberg, op. cit., p. 22. See also the article by Martin L. Kilson in the same volume for the case of Sierra Leone.

35 Aristide R. Zolberg, 'Ivory Coast', in Coleman and Rosberg, op. cit., p. 79; Peter Harries-Jones, *Freedom and Labour. Mobilization and Political Control on the Zambian Copperbelt* (Oxford, 1975).

36 Aristide R. Zolberg, *Creating Political Order. The Party-States of West Africa* (Chicago, 1966), p. 15.

37 See Mamdani, op. cit., for a detailed discussion of the failure of the petty bourgeoisie to emerge as an integrated and unified class during the colonial period in Uganda.

38 See René Lemarchand, 'Political Clientelism and Ethnicity in Tropical Africa: Competing Solidarities in Nation-Building', *American Political Science Review*, 66, 1 (1972), pp. 68–90 for an elaboration of this argument.

39 Howard Wolpe, *Urban Politics in Nigeria. A Study of Port Harcourt* (Berkeley, 1974), p. 118.

40 Julius K. Nyerere, *Freedom and Socialism: A Selection from Writings and Speeches 1965–1967* (Dar es Salaam, 1968), p. 27.

41 Kwame Nkrumah, *Dark Days in Ghana* (London, 1968), p. 71.

42 For a similar argument, see Victor T. LeVine, *Political Corruption. The Ghana Case* (Stanford, 1975), pp. 86–90.

43 Sir Andrew Cohen, *British Policy in Changing Africa* (London, 1959), pp. 59–62.

44 For Cameroun see Richard A. Joseph, *Radical Nationalism in Cameroun. Social Origins of the UPC Rebellion* (Oxford, 1977). For Kenya, see Odinga, op. cit., pp. 256–7; and Gary Wasserman, *Politics of Decolonisation. Kenya Europeans and the Land Issue 1960–1965* (Cambridge, 1976).

45 John S. Saul, 'The Revolution in Portugal's African Colonies; A Review Essay', *Canadian Journal of African Studies*, 9, 2 (1975), p. 330.

46 Nyerere, op. cit., pp. 27, 28.

47 For a discussion of the differences between conventional nationalism of the late 1950s and early 1960s and revolutionary nationalism in Mozambique in the 1970s, see John S. Saul, 'Frelimo and the Mozambique Revolution', in Giovanni Arrighi and John S. Saul, eds., *Essays on the Political Economy of Africa* (New York, 1973), pp. 379–86.

48 Samora Machel, *Establishing People's Power to Serve the Masses* (Dar es Salaam, 1977), p. 2.

2 Conflict, Coalitions and Coups

To us, their mandate is simply a license to profiteer.
Sembene Ousmane, *God's Bits of Wood* (London, 1970).

Governmental and political positions within the state apparatus have been ardently sought after in all African countries since independence. The reasons why office has been so keenly desired are various but are doubtless connected with questions of power and wealth. But the number of political and governmental positions available to meet the demands of the large numbers of aspirants is limited. Competition for office – both within the ruling party as well as from opposition parties – has consequently been intense. Aspirant politicians have organized themselves in their quest for power and economic resources and have resorted to various stratagems – patron–client relations, manipulation of sectional (especially ethnic) loyalties – as well as to such stratagems as ballot-rigging, coercion and intimidation, to attain and retain office. Military coups have often been connected with this competition and struggle for office. But the new military rulers, just like their civilian predecessors, have used their office to enhance their personal power and privilege. It is this competition and struggle for power and wealth amongst Africa's state personnel since independence that is the subject of the present chapter.*

Conflict

The nationalist party which became the ruling party at the time of independence was, in essence, a collection of disparate leaders and their respective followings. Shortly after independence, and in some African countries even before independence, the diversity of the political leadership led to divisions within the new governing party. Ideological,

* An earlier version of this chapter was published as 'Servir ou se servir? Commentaires a partir du Sierra Leone', *Politique Africaine*, No. 6 (1982), pp. 5–18.

personality and ethnic differences all led to discord. But most intra-party disputes were less concerned with such differences which were, in fact, variants of the main cause of cleavage. The political leaders conflicted with each other primarily over securing and maintaining positions of power and influence in the government and party. Party struggles were rarely based on broad social divisions but were largely personal or factional divisions over office-holding.

Governmental and political party positions, at central as well as local levels, were keenly sought after as a means to secure participation in decision-making and the distribution of the benefits of power. Control of political and government office was clearly seen as bringing with it control over the channels of decision-making, over the allocation of scarce resources (such as contracts, loans, jobs or business licences) as well as providing opportunities for material gain. It is the use of political and government office for individual accumulation that we especially wish to emphasize. The pursuit of cash and happiness is a key motivation for seeking office and needs to be stressed. Politics, as the drafters of the recent Nigerian constitutional proposals reminded us, revolves signifi-cantly around gaining the 'opportunity to acquire wealth and prestige and to be able to distribute benefits in the form of jobs, contracts, scholarships and gifts of money and so on to one's relatives and political allies'.[1]

Even during the colonial period, most notably in territories such as the Gold Coast and Nigeria, politics was regarded by many as a commercial venture in its own right. Public office was viewed as facilitating private gain. Writing about the nationalist politicians, one writer has commented:

> In addition to satisfying individual or psychic needs, political office provided a schoolteacher or clerk with his only likely opportunity for personal financial advancement. A successful candidate for parliament would easily quintuple his salary and would have access to means for taking care of his extended family's needs and desires. Like most successful politicians anywhere, these men were truly hungry for office.[2]

Since independence, leadership positions have continued to be highly valued, particularly because of the financial rewards of office-holding. At all levels of the party and government apparatus – national as well as local – the incumbents of office have expected to earn high salaries, often many times higher than the earnings of peasants and workers, even without taking into account their car allowances, housing subsidies and other emoluments. On top of this have been the earnings possible from the use of office for private gain – such as through favouritism (in the award of contracts or licences) or through the diversion of public funds into private accounts. In some African countries the political leadership has been especially venal and rapacious, but throughout sub-Saharan Africa office-holding has been coveted as a major way by which politicians can improve their economic and social positions. Political and government office has been clearly marked out as a springboard for individual enrichment.

Partaking of the spoils afforded by political office stems from various motivations. Memories of the deprivation suffered by politicians during the colonial period has doubtless been an important psychological factor. Political leaders in most of black Africa hoped that the acquisition of political power would serve to overcome the frustrations they experienced under colonialism. By acquiring political control, the leadership hoped to attain the rewards previously denied it. Another motivation has been that connected with the insecurity under which the incumbents of political power have operated since independence. Political insecurity, stemming from several factors, has ensured that politicians would be especially concerned with the use of political office for private advantage. But perhaps Nyerere's views, as indicated in the previous chapter, provide the key explanation for the manifestly acquisitive propensities of Africa's politicians: 'they wished to use positions of power for private gain, because almost the only way in which Africans could get the capital to become landlords or capitalists was by virtue of their office or their seniority in the public service'.[3] Personal accumulation was motivated by a personal desire for the fruits of capitalism. State personnel – political leaders and civil servants – desired to transcend their marginal economic position. As the more profitable avenues of economic enterprise were occupied by foreign capital, the only other way to accumulate wealth, apart from trade, was through government and politics. Access to the spoils of office would provide politicians with the means to acquire business interests and property and enhance their move into the class of propertied owners. Political office and state power was therefore the key by which a petty bourgeoisie could transform itself into a property-owning bourgeoisie.

But the number of political offices (such as those of ministers, party executives, parliamentarians, chiefs, or local councillors) to absorb the large number of aspirants was limited. Competition for political office has consequently been fierce and, at times, bitter, and examples in contemporary Africa are legion. All ruling parties have experienced internal tensions and in many the process of intra-party competition has resulted in serious turmoil as rival party politicians have struggled either to attain or to retain the limited number of positions available.

An example of a dramatic and significant manifestation of such competition occurred in Zambia at the elections for the fifteen members of the ruling United National Independence Party Central Committee in August 1967. Factional competition between the different leaders in UNIP over the allocation of position and influence was so intense that party unity and political stability were seriously threatened. In Kenya the ruling party, KANU, has been plagued by continual factional conflicts, especially at the local level but also within the national leadership, as rival politicians have struggled to acquire or retain political office.

But in spite of the warring factionalism within governing parties, it is important to note a striking feature of African politics, namely, the relative cohesion of the ruling group in the maintenance of state power. The ruling group has been able to integrate the different politicians within the ruling circle and effect a considerable degree of political consolidation. Cohesion has been fostered so that all the leaders work together within the party and the government. Such cohesion may be the result of short-term material gains; individuals join the ruling coalition because of the jobs, loans, contracts, economic aid, and so forth that they actually receive or are promised. Occasionally, the benefits of government are not the only possible way of preserving elite cohesion. Ideology can link the leaders. Few parties in Africa, however, have been unified by the compulsions of doctrine. In most cases elite integration has been mainly the end-product of the allocation of patronage and spoils. As O'Brien noted of the Union Progressiste Sénégalaise (UPS) in the 1960s: 'Many who have joined the governing party have done so purely in order to enjoy the fruits of government, and are committed to no programme other than their own advancement.'[4]

Nevertheless, given the relative scarcity of patronage and spoils, political strife within the ruling party has continued to prevail and elite cohesion has remained rather tenuous. In addition to intra-governing party cleavages, inter-party conflict has been a major source of political competition in Africa. Competition has not only occurred within the dominant party for positions of power and influence but also between rival political parties as members of competing parties have engaged in a struggle for control of state power. As we have noted, the state possesses control over the distribution of goods and services and it is therefore not surprising that politicians – both within the ruling as well as opposition parties – seek to exert influence over the process by occupying public office and official position. However, as we have also argued, positions of leadership are highly prized mainly because of the material and pecuniary benefits office-holding brings to its occupants. Opposition politicans as well have wanted to acquire those positions within the state apparatus primarily to advance their own personal interests and further individual accumulation.

Politics in Africa has revolved significantly around the desire of politicians to gain office and to hold on to it as tightly as possible. At the same time those not in office have sought to attain positions of leadership. The reasons why political office at all levels is so keenly desired (and why competition for office is so frantic) are various but doubtless the status and income attainable from the post as well as the capacity to acquire property and join the bourgeoisie are prime motivations to office-holding. Cohen has shown how the 'politico-administrative class' in the Ivory Coast 'has managed to obtain a disproportionate share of urban resources such as land, housing, education, jobs, and social services'[5] and his argument applies equally to both urban and rural resources and opportunities elsewhere in Africa. As the saying goes in Zambia, 'It pays to join UNIP'; indeed, it pays to attain political and government office.

Politicians and bureaucrats have used state resources to enhance their personal fortunes as well as to enhance their individual mobility. This has, however, not always entailed an illegal process. State personnel have been in a favoured position to gain access to loans, licences and contracts. Yet the temptations of power are great. Although it has to be acknowledged that leaders in some countries are renowned for their self-sacrifice and puritanism, nevertheless manipulation of political office through illegal means for personal enrichment has proven to be a feature characteristic of politicians and officials in black Africa. Ruth First has described how Nigeria's First Republic 'became an orgy of power being turned to profit', while the Gowon years, 1970–5, were ones when 'corruption reached new peaks as public life became infected by moral squalor and financial acquisitiveness'.[6] Similarly in other African countries party leaders have waxed prosperous in office. As Dr Kofi Busia admitted whilst he was prime minister of Ghana: 'There is not a single honest person in my Cabinet.'[7] Or, as President Mobutu declared about his country where corruption abounds: 'In Zaire everything is for sale.'[8] Mobutu himself is known to have personal wealth running in billions of dollars, while Zaire is destitute. During his fourteen years in power in the Central African Republic, self-proclaimed Emperor Jean Bédel Bokassa acquired chateaux and fashionable restaurants in France with public money and was known to have directed external aid to his accounts in Switzerland. His extravagant coronation in 1977 alone cost Ł12 million in a country where total revenues were only Ł14 million. Even in those few countries such as Tanzania and Zambia where the government has sought to curb private accumulation by leaders (through such devices as the Leadership Code), the atittude of *enrichessez-vous*, although checked, has persisted. 'Almost all leaders want money and are being bribed,' the Tanzanian president is reported as having stated.[9] In Zambia, too, in the light of revelations about irregular behaviour by top government officials and politicans, there can be little doubt about some corrupt practices. A country such as Guinea, where the evils of private wealth and the need for new socialist men and women is stressed, has also not been exempt: 'a schizophrenic blend of personal corruption and socialist militancy' is how one writer has described the situation there.[10] But in such countries as Mozambique, Guinea, Tanzania and Zambia, for instance, the pickings would seem to have been comparatively modest. To be sure office has everywhere been an avenue to material well-being but only in the more capitalist-type systems (such as those in

Kenya, Nigeria and Zaire) would it appear that it has also been an avenue to great wealth.

Coalitions

In their quest for power and influence, political rivals have organized themselves for competition and struggle. To advance their interests as against those of their opponents, aspiring politicians have sought to establish bases of support in particular local institutions (rural and urban government, co-operatives) and organizations (trade unions, parastatals, military). Networks of alliances extending from politicians at all levels of the political system to followers in various social groups and localities have been readily observable in most African countries. Such coalitions providing specific bases of support have then been available for use by politicians in contests for power.[11]

Politicians have penetrated institutions and organizations both to extend their own support as well as to undermine that of their rivals for power. Various associations have been drawn into politics owing to the political resources they control and the fact that these organizational resources can be translated into political influence and political position for those contending for power. Sandbrook has shown why the trade-union movement in Kenya was drawn into politics. It provided, he writes, 'a ready-made, poly-ethnic, territory-wide, organisational network for any politician who wished to establish his own political machine . . . he who controlled the labour movement had power over a significant proportion of the politically-relevant strata in Kenya [which] . . . would be invaluable in any election or intra-party contest'.[12] Power struggles within or between parties have also resulted in the main contenders penetrating local political arenas. As we shall attempt to show in our case-study on Sierra Leone, such penetration was undertaken to maintain or eliminate the political base of a particular party or intra-party faction.

These coalitions, especially those between governing party politicians and their followers, have been based on a reciprocal relationship. Politicians have provided or promised to provide aid in the form of both material and non-material resources. Those who have been in positions of power have been able to dispense goods and services and to distribute largesse to selective clients in order to attract and maintain support. Resort by politicians to patronage – entailing favouritism in the award of loans, licences, contracts, jobs, scholarships, roads, schools, clinics, water supplies and the like – has been an important means of organizing political backing. Their rivals, either within the same party or in opposition parties, although limited in their access to material resources, have been able to muster support, albeit with difficulty, on the basis of promises of patronage in the future. Non-material payoffs have also been of importance. For example, political leaders have sought to assist their followers in either gaining or retaining office in the associations and localities. Politicians have manipulated appointments to public boards and corporations as well as influenced the dismissal of holders of public office. Once again those in control of government have been best placed to favour their supporters at the expense of opponents. The clients have reciprocated the benefits received from their patrons with more intangible assets, such as demonstrations of allegiance and esteem, information on the machinations of a patron's enemies, and partisan support, especially at times of elections or intra-party struggles. Maxwell Owusu has shown how status, jobs, and material benefits held together the leaders and the led in Swedru in the Central Region of Ghana during the 1950s and 1960s. He writes:

> The relationship between leaders and followers tends to be personal, yet significantly utilitarian. Political commitment, therefore, is primarily instrumental. Leaders confer political office and status, and – for their active followers – public employment. Subordinate leaders and their followers who are rewarded by the system make payments in the form of votes and other modes of support for the system. Ghanaian political leaders are thus chiefly accountable to their followers and the general public for private, utilitarian stakes.[13]

A further stratagem employed by politicians in the interest of their own political advancement has entailed the deliberate manipulation of sectional loyalties among the masses. In their appeals for support, sectional divisions within society have been exploited. A symbiotic relationship has emerged between politicians, who desire to further their own positions, and their 'people', who are fearful of domination (economic and political) by a culturally distinct group allegedly organized for these ends.

In a context of cultural pluralism as prevails in most African countries, it is not surprising that ethnic appeals have struck the most responsive chord among the masses. Most politicians have attempted to exploit ethnic loyalties to further their own political ends. Although all political leaders have publicly denounced the notion of 'tribalism' in the most stringent terms, they have nevertheless continued to foster it in order to muster political support. Aspirant politicians have defined themselves as the representatives of communal interests and have been able to rally support for their own interests by means of 'tribalistic' demagogy and/or the promise of benefits and rewards to those with whom they share ethnic ties.

Examples of this stimulation of ethnic loyalties by politicians are innumerable. One case, already mentioned, was that involving conflicts amongst Zambia's UNIP party leaders, who fomented sectional conflict in 1967 to obtain political support for their own ends. Conflict, Molteno maintains, revolved around political office (and, consequently, the spoils that could be obtained), but was expressed in sectional terms. Sectional leaders fostered sectional identities by playing on the emotions of their followers to win political support.[14]

A number of points relating to the notion of 'tribalism' in African politics are worthy of note. First, the mere existence within a single country of diverse ethnic groups does not imply the necessity of ethnic conflict; 'tribalism' is a loyalty or identity which can be politicized only under certain specifiable conditions. Conflict among aspirant politicians, ensuing from competition over the distribution of power and economic resources, produces 'tribalism' rather than 'tribalism' being the cause of conflict. From this perspective, as Howard Wolpe has expressed it, 'tribalism' is not 'an independent political force in its own right . . . but rather the channel through which other interests are directed and made manifest'.[15] Wolpe has shown in his study of the city of Port Harcourt in Nigeria how virtually all ethnic conflicts have been rooted in the competition between individuals for the scarce resources of wealth, status and power. Thus conflict between Igbo and non-Igbo communities was traceable not to linguistic and cultural differences but rather to a struggle for control of Port Harcourt and the city's important economic resources. Ethnic conflict was sparked by those for whom 'tribalism' was a weapon in their struggle for political advancement.[16] As Amílcar Cabral once said: 'there are no real conflicts between the peoples of Africa. There are only conflicts between their elites'. Or, to quote the comments of a former Zairean diplomat which summarize neatly our present argument: politics, he claimed,

> is no longer a means of gaining power to serve the people and the State, but a quick way of getting rich. And since it is a profession which appears to require little intellectual preparation, the number of professional politicians has been on the increase. Often these people come from widely diversified milieux, from different regions and different tribes. As a result of these particular circumstances, most of the political crises . . . are, in fact, personal conflicts between these professional politicians and do not reflect the reactions of the Congolese masses.[17]

All persons possess multiple social identities, whether they are ethnic, clan, religious or socio-economic. These social identities are of varying salience depending upon the perception of the situation with which people are confronted. This fact influences political behaviour. Politicians employ sectional loyalties situationally. When leaders are competing at the national level, as was the case in the Central Committee elections of UNIP in 1967, they appeal to ethnic or provincial loyalty to rally support. When the arena of competition is within the province composed of people from all the same ethnic group, then, in order to win support, they appeal to smaller sectional loyalties than the ethnic or provincial group, such as to chiefdom or clan identities.

In their attempts to mobilize popular support, a number of African regimes have undertaken 'cultural revolutions', so-called, which have been essentially a series of decrees directed at expunging alien practices and influences in the countries concerned. Inspired in part in recent times by President Mobutu of Zaire, these cultural revolutions (also referred to as 'authenticité' campaigns) have become important weapons restoring the image of governing parties on the decline. President Tombalbaye attempted to revive the sagging fortunes of the PPT (Parti Progressiste Tchadien) to its former radical image.

> by including a variety of symbolic gestures, policies and edicts calculated to appeal to various strata of society vital to the regime's survival. Thus, the numerous foreign-policy shifts . . . were aimed at urban youth and intellectuals chaffing at Chad's extremely docile international stances. The reimposition of the Yondo initiation rites . . . was likewise an immensely popular move among traditionalists in the countryside, while fitting well with Tombalbaye's new 'nationalist' image.[18]

Elsewhere in Africa, political leaders have revived xenophobia to restore the sagging prestige of their regimes. The following description of the harassment of Asians is revealing of attacks on this minority in Eastern Africa:

> Nowadays, the Asian is portrayed as little more than a miserly/duka-wallah who ceaselessly exploited and cheated innocent Africans. His past distorted, he is in the process of being eliminated from the present. With predictable and tiresome regularity one politician or another will rise to his feet in the Assembly and demand the liquidation of the surviving 'little Bombays' – that is the ritual phrase used to describe the lingering concentrations of Asian business enterprise. In a survey of Nairobi's industrial development (published as a supplement by the *Nation*) there was no mention made of Asian entrepreneurial and technical skills.[19]

President Amin's attack on the Asian community of Uganda in the early 1970s was especially designed to invoke collective support. The expulsion of Asians was favourably greeted by the African population and did much to broaden Amin's popular constituency as well as consolidate his political position. Popular support has also been evoked as a result of attacks on foreign Africans. A government under pressure has usually been assured of a short reprieve by expelling a symbolic number of Dahomeans, Togolese or Igbos. The Busia government, for example, in order to prop up its shaky position, enacted legislation in 1970 which exiled a large number (nearly one hundred thousand) of non-nationals who had traditionally lived and worked in Ghana. And, similarly, the expulsion of two million or more foreign Africans, predominantly Ghanaians, from Nigeria in 1983 'is the Nigerian president's xenophobic way of courting votes in next summer's election at a time when his country's economy is in well-deserved tatters'.[20]

The possibility for politicians to organize themselves for competition and struggle has been a short-lived experience in much of post-colonial Africa. In country after country, those in control of government have used public power to preserve the political hegemony of the incumbent regime. The full panoply of state power has been brought to bear on opposition elements. Members of the ruling party have resorted to various pressures to hinder politicians from the opposition parties as well as to distort competitive politics. The existence of ballot-rigging and other election falsifications, as well as coercion, intimidation and imprisonment of opponents has been widely noted throughout Africa, as has the occasional liquidiation of enemies. In Lesotho in 1970 Chief Jonathan and his ruling Basotho National Party tried to rig the general election; when this failed and Jonathan was defeated he declared a state of emergency and jailed the opposition leadership of the Basotho Congress Party. The post-independence case of Chad provides a particularly sinister illustration of the way governing parties have asserted their political dominance. In Chad, the discovery of various plots against the regime, both real and imagined, and the concomitant waves of arrests have been a favoured way of eliminating opposition, especially as political prisoners have at times been liquidated while being held in custody.[21] Although much less murderous, the case of Cameroun is not too dissimilar: President Ahidjo established his one-party dictatorship by crushing and suppressing the opposition as well as by less forceful absorption of other groups into the ruling party.[22] In the case of Senegal, where during the 1960s the opposition was both suppressed and absorbed into the ruling UPS, it is interesting to note that opponents were reconciled to the government by material rewards. The utilitarian nature of African politics which we have emphasized throughout this chapter is clearly evident in the following comment: 'The temptations of the fruits of office held out by President Senghor . . . proved irresistible for all but a very few.'[23] But whatever the methods employed, in nearly all African countries competitive party politics has either been terminated (with opposition parties being banned or blighted) or, if still permitted, has been severely muted or distorted. 'No other party than ZANU–PF shall ever rule in Zimbabwe' thunders Prime Minister Robert Mugabe at party meetings. Winner takes all is the rule in African politics.

The abolition of opposition parties has not, of course, meant the end of political conflict and struggle. Political divisions over the distribution of power and economic resources have now taken place within the single-party system. And in their quest for power and wealth political rivals have continued their political manoeuvres and intrigues, seeking support through their patronage networks (founded on material and non-material obligations), as well as through the manipulation of sectional ties and identities. But the political monopoly of the *parti unique* poses the problem of factional politics deteriorating into violence and instability. There is always the danger that factional politics may heighten attempts to remove those in power through plots and coups or even produce civil wars (between factions transformed into private armies – as occurred in Chad following the overthrow of Tombalbaye in 1975). To contain factionalism and to ensure that it remains within acceptable limits, those in power have resorted to various practices, which include purges and rehabilitations. Members have been expelled from the ruling group, or outcasts have been restored to membership within the ruling oligarchy. Yet situations of political monopoly cannot easily overcome the politics of uncertainty consequent upon factionalism; and conspiracies and coups have characterized contemporary African political life.

For purposes of exposition and illustration, we now present a case-study of conflict and coalitions based on the West African state of Sierra Leone.

Two major political parties – the All Peoples Congress (APC) and the Sierra Leone Peoples Party (SLPP) – have competed for national political power in contemporary Sierra Leone. The SLPP held national office from the time of independence in 1961 till 1967. The APC secured a majority over the SLPP in the 1967 general election, the first change of government through the ballot box in post-colonial Africa. Military intervention, however, prevented the peaceful transfer of national power. The military took over for thirteen months, after which, in 1968, a new APC government emerged. The APC ruled till the general election in mid-1973. At this election national political competition came to an end as a result of APC politicians and activists forcibly preventing SLPP candidates from being nominated.[24] A *de facto* one-party state was now created, with the APC being the sole party permitted to exist. In 1977, after the APC ensured once again that most SLPP candidates could not stand for election, and after the institution of a fraudulent referendum, a *de jure* one-party state was established in Sierra Leone.

The leadership of both the APC and the SLPP have employed various tactics to retain office. Retention of office in a two-party system implied success at general elections, which could be ensured in two ways. First the ruling party had to maintain party unity and support, which could be achieved through patronage. Party leaders distributed material benefits and services to party officials as well as to those sections of the electorate which favoured the party concerned. Secondly, various methods, including election-rigging, have been resorted to in order to undermine opponents. Opposition supporters in Sierra Leone have, since 1961, been harassed, intimidated, detained and even killed. New opposition parties have also been stifled at birth.[25] All of these tactics have been common in Sierra Leone since independence. The repression of opponents intensified considerably under APC rule and in the 1970s all constituted, open competition was eliminated and organized opposition was crushed.

Those who were in power have been desperate to stay in power. Most politicians possessed little wealth or capital when they acceded to political office. But political office has given them access to wealth and has become an important avenue to self-enrichment. Many, if not most, of Sierra Leone's politicians have, while in power, dipped their hands into the public till. Many of these politicians have been notorious for their corruption when in power. A commission into corruption made it clear that leading members of the SLPP, including the prime minister, Sir Albert Margai, were deeply involved in corrupt activities. During the three years he was head of government, Sir Albert received at least £200,000 beyond his lawful income and he was ordered by the commission to repay the state the sum of £771,037. The bank balances of APC ministers and party officials have also been swollen with the 'sweets of office', and the president, Siaka Stevens, has become enormously rich since taking office in 1968.[26]

In order to advance their interests and preserve their control of political office, leaders of the two major parties, especially during the period of party competition up to 1973, sought to construct alliances or coalitions with various organizations and institutions throughout Sierra Leone. The key network of alliances was that between national parties and chiefdom factions.[27] Sierra Leone is organized into numerous, independent chiefdoms at the local level. The chiefdoms, of which there are 148 today, constitute the chief focus of loyalty for the majority of the people (89 per cent of Sierra Leone's population live in chiefdoms). Whoever controlled the chiefdoms would thus have power over a very significant proportion of the country's adult population.

The chiefdom is the lowest area of political competition in Sierra Leone. Politics in the chiefdoms has been principally concerned with the acquisition or retention of control of chiefdom office. The prime post at the chiefdom level (because of its major privileges and perquisites) is that of the paramount chief. Only persons descended from a chiefly family in the chiefdom concerned are eligible to contest an election for the position of paramount chief. Almost every chiefdom has at least two 'ruling' houses and, given the lucrativeness of the post of paramount chief, there has always been active competition among rival camps for the chieftaincy. Rival competitors, drawn from a narrow stratum of the chiefdom population, have built clienteles, composed of relatives and supporters, to assist them in political competition. These conflict groups, or chiefdom factions, have been centred primarily around dynastic rivalries.[28]

There has been an intimate relationship between intra-chiefdom factions and national political parties. Since the advent of party politics in Sierra Leone during the 1950s, chiefdom factions and parties have been closely associated. The chiefdom factions were affiliated with the parties on grounds of expedience: they hoped to secure outside help in order to acquire or retain office. On the other hand, rival national parties needed allies in the chiefdoms in order to extend their own influence and organizational support. In Sierra Leone parties have been weak and febrile bodies not possessing much of an organization at the local level. They therefore courted chiefdom factions seeking alliances in order to establish a firm organizational base in the local communities.[29]

Up to 1967 the ruling SLPP worked mainly with the paramount chiefs – the chiefdom incumbents – throughout the country. Since the government party was allied with the ruling chiefdom group there was a tendency for opposition parties such as the APC to be connected with opposition or 'out' chiefdom factions. There was a continuation of the politics of alliance during the period of APC rule, 1968–73, although the alignments were less clear-cut than in the period prior to 1967. Both the governing APC and the opposition SLPP had close links with paramount chiefs and 'out' chiefdom factions. Since the ending of national party competition in mid-1973, national party–chiefdom faction alliances have persisted, albeit within a one-party situation. Rival chiefdom factions now give at least nominal support to the ruling APC but are linked more specifically with rival groups or individuals within the governing party.

During the years of inter-party competition there was a reciprocal relationship between ruling party and chiefdom faction. Ruling-party politicians strove to ensure that their chiefdom-level supporters acquired or retained their power and position. Indeed, chiefdom political struggles were considerably influenced by the central regime as parliamentarians, ministers, and even prime ministers involved themselves in chiefdom political contests. Ruling-party politicians, for example, exerted various pressures – bribery, coercion, threats – to influence who was elected chiefdom ruler. As to whether a paramount chief was deposed or not also depended on the attitude of the central regime. Since independence, political factors (such as support for an opposition party rather than, as in colonial times, the extent of chiefly misgovernment) have largely determined whether a chief has been removed from office. Tenure of chiefly office as well as accession to the chieftaincy was dependent on political-party affiliation. Generally, up to 1967, it was the factions connected to the ruling SLPP which were able to achieve their ends of procuring or preserving the chieftaincy. Moreover, deposition of paramount chiefs loyal to the governing party was hardly contemplated, even if such chiefs were highly unpopular with their people. Under APC rule as well, up to 1973, factions allied with the ruling party were likewise in a favoured position, although this was by no means automatic.[30] In addition to assistance from the ruling party in chiefdom political competition, government supporters within the chiefdoms benefited from resources at the disposal of the central regime such as water supplies, roads, medical services, or loans.

On the other hand chiefdom factions worked for the government party, particularly at election time. The major parties concluded alliances with segments within the chiefdoms, which they hoped would make up for their organizational deficiencies. At election time, the parties relied on chiefdom factions for almost all political organizational work such as raising funds, conducting election campaigns and vote-getting. Competition between parties was expressed in terms of conflict between chiefdom factions, and electoral campaigns developed along the lines of internal cleavage in the chiefdom. Moreover, political party affiliation in an election was largely determined by factional association.[31] Faction leaders converted their faction into a 'vote bank' for a particular party, while the majority of the ordinary people probably voted for a party on the basis of their relations with one or other faction, rather than according to any personal political convictions.

It is also the case, however, that identification with a political party was based on loyalty to an ethnic group. To some extent political parties have emphasized ethnic (and regional) differences. Up to 1967 the APC enjoyed a large base of support in the north, while the SLPP predominated in the south. The northern peoples had become increasingly aware of their province as a neglected region, while the SLPP government appeared to favour the southern Mende areas. Economic benefits (public projects and public funds) were alleged to be enjoyed more in the south and there was an acute sense of regional deprivation amongst the northern peoples. The APC, it has been argued, was able to exploit this consciousness by appealing to regionalism and by promising a reallocation of public resources.[32] But SLPP leaders also appealed for support on the basis of their regional identification. The SLPP prime minister, Sir Albert Margai, manipulated ethnic imagery with a particular vehemence, charging that a 'Temne–Creole axis' which constituted the APC would 'cut the Mende man's throat' if it was elected to power.[33]

Before the 1967 general election, therefore, politicians at the national level appealed for support by manipulating ethnic and regional sentiments among the masses. But when, during the election, the arena of competition was at the local level, an appeal was made to smaller sectional loyalties. This was because party competition in the constituencies was between local persons. SLPP and APC candidates stood in their constituencies of origin and local cleavages were perceived as being important as a means of aggregating support. And, as a result, alliances fashioned between national parties and chiefdom factions became significant.

But these central–local alliances have been constituted on grounds of expedience. Weak party commitment has meant that chiefdom factions have at times changed their party ties, especially when they felt their local interests would be better served in an alliance with a different party. The volatility of party ties should not be overstressed, but given a fairly weak party solidarity, national politics becomes unstable whenever party leaders are unable to rely on their local clients. It was fear of the fragility of the SLPP that led the prime minister to make plans for the establishment of a one-party state in 1966. His failure to create a one-party state, coupled with the departure of a number of chiefdom factions from the SLPP fold (especially in the south), led to the downfall of his government in the 1967 general election. It was to prevent further transfer of party allegiance, following splintering in the APC in 1970, that led the new prime minister, Siaka Stevens, to seek to eliminate opposition parties in the 1970s and to prevent the SLPP from nominating candidates in the 1973 and 1977 general elections. But political monopoly has not ended political instability and factionalism and conspiracy have plagued the APC ruling group.

Coups

Military intervention in sub-Saharan Africa has often been seen as emanating from the inadequacies of civilian rule. Coups have occurred, it has been argued, as the military have sought to overthrow corrupt, inefficient or venal civilian regimes. Recent research, however, has provided more complex explanations of army takeovers in Africa. This has shown that although coups are reflections of disputes within the civilian elites, they ensue primarily from links between military and civilian elite groups. As Thomas Cox has demonstrated in his study of military takeovers in Sierra Leone, 'it is within this rather complex spectrum of civilian and military intercourse that the actual preconditions for intervention are established'.[34] A study of military intervention in Sierra Leone may be rewarding for the insights it provides into army coups elsewhere in Africa.

As elsewhere on the continent, members of the first ruling party in independent Sierra Leone – the Sierra Leone People's Party (SLPP) – were determined to entrench themselves in power in order to protect their personal interests. If their privileges were to be safeguarded, then the political leadership had to devise a means of asserting effective control over the military. The prime minister, Sir Albert Margai, was especially concerned with achieving civilian control over the armed forces. The coups d'état in neighbouring West African countries, particularly those in Nigeria and Ghana in 1966, must have demonstrated to him the inherent fragility of civilian regimes unable to maintain control over their armies. And given a situation of mounting opposition to his domestic programmes, coupled with the fear of possible anti-government sentiments within certain sections of the army, Sir Albert began to develop mechanisms of control over his armed forces, designed especially to link members of the SLPP ruling circle to senior military officers. By developing close links between the ruling civilian politicians and military officers, the political leadership hoped to preserve itself in power.

Sir Albert's method of control envisaged 'the consolidation of civilian and military elites, with a pivotal role being reserved for the force commander'.[35] The force commander, David Lansana, became an intimate associate of Sir Albert's clique within the SLPP. Moreover, SLPP leaders sought to bring as many members of the officer corps as possible into the fold of the ruling party. The result was a coalition of civilian and military elites in a network of elite relationships. The bonds between army officers and members of the SLPP executive were forged primarily through common ethnic (Mende) and regional (Moyamba District) identity, but also included extended family relationships and secondary-school affiliations. Cox shows how the prime minister and his force commander, concerned to create a Mende-controlled army, began to make tribal affiliation the key basis for recruitment to the officer corps. By packing the army with Mendes they hoped to 'guarantee SLPP control of the army well into the future'.[36] By early 1967 the Mende proportion of the entire officer corps was estimated to have reached approximately 52 per cent, well over the Mende proportion of the population as a whole. Cox's summary of the growing fusion of civilian politicians and military officers is worth quoting at length, as it demonstrates the mutually beneficial nature of the links between these groups:

> On the most elementary level, a common ethnic and regional identity helped fashion an allegiance between army officers and civilian influentials once Mendes came to predominate in the upper echelons of both sectors. Client–patron ties between army small boys and civilian big men – facilitated by the close physical proximity of army barracks and ministerial quarters in Freetown – also helped mediate civil–military interaction and eventually allowed for the development of a kind of symbiotic relationship between the two elites. The army officers needed identification with prominent civilians to raise the former's status in the wider community and, indirectly, to further their military careers. The politicians required the assurance that in the event they could no longer hold the public trust, the army, guns drawn, would remain at their sides.[37]

The failure of the SLPP's efforts at civilian control of the army was brought dramatically to the fore by the military intervention of March 1967.[38] The military upheavals of 1967 were, as we shall suggest below, the end product of internal power struggles within the army, onto which were grafted disputes among civilian politicians.

During the year prior to the March 1967 coup there were serious tensions within the officer corps of the Royal Sierra Leone Military Forces. Cox writes: 'ethnicity, promotional anxieties, and other socio-political factors were at the heart of the challenge to Lansana's authority, [and] these issues were reinforced by bickering over perceived grievances of a highly personal nature'.[39] Lansana was in conflict with a group of officers, including John Bangura, whose sympathies lay with the opposition party, the All Peoples Congress (APC). This intra-army fragmentation coincided with inter-party political conflict (APC against SLPP) as well as intra-party struggles within the SLPP (those for or against Sir Albert). Each of the various political groups was linked with certain army cliques. The army cliques were thus politicized. In February 1967 Colonel Bangura and seven other officers were arrested on the charge of plotting to overthrow the government.

When the SLPP lost the general election in March 1967, it was clear that Lansana's intervention was necessary to defend and rescue the ruling circle of Sir Albert Margai. A counter-coup a few days later, led by a group of anti-Lansana military officers, ousted the force commander and installed a military regime styled the National Reformation Council. These army upheavals of 1967 cannot be adequately explained by the sorts of factors usually cited in the literature on military intervention into the political arena. Factors such as the faltering economy and the avaricious and self-seeking nature of politicians are not much validity in the Sierra Leonean case. They may constitute the 'backdrop' against which coups occur. But the prime reason why Brigadier Lansana struck was because he 'found himself obligated, by dint of his relationship to Sir Albert and the SLPP, to defend the ruling circle at any cost . . .'.[40]

A year later, in April 1968, the military regime was overthrown. A small group of warrant officers and NCOs acting on behalf of the army privates ousted the military government and restored civilian rule. The privates' mutiny was the result of serious discontent within the lower echelons of the army. During the period of rule by the National Reformation Council the rank and file in the army were badly neglected. Resentment on the part of discontented soldiers was thus a key motive in producing the 1968 coup.

The new civilian APC government, under Siaka Stevens, was also concerned to develop an effective means of civilian control of the army. Within two months of his accession to office, Stevens had purged the officer corps of several officers and warrant officers alleged to be closely involved with some SLPP politicians. Most of the officers removed were Mendes who, because of their tribal affiliations, were seen as potentially untrustworthy to the regime in power. The purged officers were replaced by northerners of various tribes (mainly Temnes and Limbas). Additional tactics were employed by Stevens, such as the approval of a substantial increase in military expenditure, construction of new barracks and the replacement of outdated weapons.

But just as tensions within the armed forces in the mid-1960s, often revolving around the Lansana–Bangura rivalry, had led to fragmentation of the officer corps, so rivalries between John Bangura and Joseph Saidu Momoh resulted in cleavages among members of the senior command in the late 1960s and 1970s. Colonel Bangura, a part-Temne, was the force commander while Lieutenant-Colonel Momoh, a Limba, was the commander of the first battalion. Momoh shared a common tribal identity with Siaka Stevens and 'was known to be circumventing the line of command to court the prime minister's personal favour';[41] while Bangura was alleged to have sympathies with one of the opposition parties, the United Democratic Party (UDP), a breakaway movement from the APC. In 1967 the Lansana–Bangura rivalry had been exacerbated by the struggles between the APC and the SLPP. In 1970 feuding between the APC and the UDP inflamed relations between Bangura and Momoh. Cox writes; 'As in 1967, intra-civilian fragmentation now coincided with intra-army fragmentation, and the stage was set once again for a revival of military praetorianism.'[42]

In March 1971 Bangura staged a coup which proved to be abortive. Bangura was executed and replaced by Momoh as force commander. Since then Stevens has resorted to various tactics to preserve civilian control of the army and ensure physical protection against his internal opponents. He has nurtured pro-APC cliques of officers and has set up, with Cuban assistance, the Internal Security Unit (ISU) which, although a component of the police force, is clearly a countervailing force to the regular army. These tactics have served to perpetuate Stevens in power. But there are no certain guarantees that military intervention will not occur (various military plots have been foiled) 'as long as civilian cliques persist in feuding among themselves and as long as this behaviour is mirrored in the army'.[43]

Military coups in Africa which have toppled civilian governments have often been attributed to the corruption and venality of civilian regimes. It may well be the case that coups have generally occurred within the context of economic crisis and corruption. But these failings of civilian leadership are not the prime causes of army takeovers. More cogent reasons for coups are concerned with personal fears and ambitions as well as corporate grievances of military men.[44] Our case-study of Sierra Leone has sought to show that personal reasons underlay most military upheavals in that country. The development of cleavages within the army and the links between conflicting army groups and competing civilian groups (concerned with attaining or retaining power) constituted the basis for military intervention for particularistic and personal reasons rather than to overthrow corrupt and inefficient civilian regimes. Decalo has emphasized the important role that personal factors have played in propelling the armed forces into the political arena, although he has tended to concern himself solely with the personal fears or ambitions of specific key officers. Cox's study, however, has demonstrated that personal tensions and ambitions among both military and civilian elites as well as interaction between cliques of the two elites were directly instrumental in sparking off attempted takeovers. Admittedly the cause of military intervention is not in all cases the same. But a better understanding of the motives behind the army coups, along the lines we have indicated, also provides insights into the nature of army rule in Africa.

Once a particular clique of officers is in power, the military government does not act in ways all that different from its civilian counterpart. A prime characteristic of army rulers which they have shared with civilian rulers has been their overriding preoccupation with personal and/or corporate aggrandisement. Decalo argues that one of the most significant outcomes of military rule has been 'the satisfaction of the personal and group grievances of the dominant officer clique'.[45] Given the personal motives for army coups in Africa, it should not come as too much of a surprise that army officers have been given to self-enrichment while in political office.[46] But, as we have sought to show in this chapter, the power elite in much of Africa has exploited its tenure of political office to its own personal advantage. Such a conclusion is now becoming a common one. After reviewing a number of case studies of military government in Africa and elsewhere in the underdeveloped world, one writer declares that 'it is clear that the enhancement of personal power and wealth is a very high priority for a large number of Third-World coup leaders'. And she concludes: 'In broad terms, the interests of military elites are the same as those of civilian elites: to enhance their power and their financial position.'[47]

NOTES

1   Quoted in Gavin Williams and Terisa Turner, 'Nigeria', in John Dunn (ed.), *West African States. Failure and Promise* (Cambridge, 1978), p. 133.
2   William J. Foltz, 'Political Opposition in Single-Party States of Tropical Africa', in Robert A. Dahl (ed.), *Regimes and Oppositions* (New Haven, 1973), p. 148.
3   Julius K. Nyerere, *Freedom and Socialism: A Selection from Writings and Speeches 1965–67* (Dar es Salaam, 1968), pp. 28–9.
4   Donal Cruise O'Brien, 'Political Opposition in Senegal: 1960–67', *Government and Opposition*, 2, 4 (1967), p. 148.

5 Michael A. Cohen, *Urban Policy and Political Conflict in Africa. A Study of the Ivory Coast* (Chicago, 1974), Chap. 3. The quote is from p. 62.

6 Ruth First, *The Barrel of a Gun. Political Power in Africa and the Coup d'Etat* (Harmondsworth, 1970), p. 102; *New African Year Book 1980* (London, 1980), p. 258; and Billy J. Dudley, *An Introduction to Nigerian Government and Politics* (London, 1982), pp. 116–20.

7 Quoted in Richard Jeffries, *Class, Power and Ideology in Ghana: the Railwaymen of Sekondi-Takoradi* (Cambridge, 1978), p. 125. In Ghana as well as in some other African countries, investigations have followed in the wake of the regimes that have fallen and these have published disclosures of the illegal financial dealings of politicians and officials. See here, for instance, Victor T. Le Vine, *Political Corruption: The Ghana Case* (Stanford, 1975).

8 Quoted in Thomas Turner, 'Mobutu's Zaire: Permanently on the Verge of Collapse?', *Current History*, 80, 464 (1981), p. 125.

9 President Nyerere as quoted in the *Sunday News* (Dar es Salaam), 24 January 1982.

10 R. W. Johnson, 'Guinea', in Dunn, op. cit., p. 50.

11 See Richard Sandbrook, 'Patrons, Clients, and Factions: New Dimensions of Conflict Analysis in Africa', *Canadian Journal of Political Science*, 5, 1 (1972), pp. 104–19.

12 Richard Sandbrook, 'Patrons, Clients, and Unions: The Labour Movement and Political Conflict in Kenya', *Journal of Commonwealth Political Studies*, 10, 1 (1972), p. 5.

13 Maxwell Owusu, 'Politics in Swedru', in Dennis Austin and Robin Luckham (eds.), *Politicians and Soldiers in Ghana 1966–1972* (London, 1975), p. 239. See also Maxwell Owusu, *Uses and Abuses of Political Power. A Case Study of Continuity and Change in the Politics of Ghana* (Chicago, 1970), where he argues that the pursuit of political power in Ghana was motivated by the desire to enhance material and status opportunities.

14 Robert Molteno, 'Cleavage and Conflict in Zambian Politics: A Study in Sectionalism', in William Tordoff (ed.), *Politics in Zambia* (Manchester, 1974), pp. 62–106.

15 Howard Wolpe, *Urban Politics in Nigeria. A Study of Port Harcourt* (Berkeley, 1974), p. 233.

16 ibid., especially pp. 232–3.

17 T. R. Kanza, 'The Problems of the Congo', *African Affairs*, 67, 266 (1968), p. 59.

18 Samuel Decalo, 'Regionalism, Political Decay, and Civil Strife in Chad', *Journal of Modern African Studies*, 18, 1 (1980), p. 48.

19 Shiva Naipaul, *North of South. An African Journey* (London, 1978), p. 77.

20 *The Economist* (London), 5 February 1983, p. 13.

21 'As was discovered after [President] Tombalbaye's fall and the release of all prisoners, at least 33 were liquidated while in custody'. Decalo, op. cit., p. 38.

22 Richard Joseph (ed.), *Gaullist Africa: Cameroon under Ahmadu Ahidjo* (Enugu, 1978).

23 O'Brien, op. cit., p. 561.

24   For a brief discussion of this election, see *The Times* (London), 30 May, 1973.
25   Christopher Allen, 'Sierra Leone', in Dunn, op. cit., pp. 196–200.
26   ibid., pp. 203–5.
27   Roger Tangri, 'Central–Local Politics in Contemporary Sierra Leone', *African Affairs*, 77, 307 (1978), pp. 165–73.
28   ibid. See also Roger Tangri, 'Paramount Chiefs and Central Governments in Sierra Leone', *African Studies*, 39, 2 (1980), pp. 183–95.
29   Walter L. Barrows, *Grassroots Politics in an African State: Integration and Development in Sierra Leone* (New York, 1976), Chap. 5.
30   Roger Tangri, 'Local Political Competition and National Politicians in Contemporary Sierra Leone', unpublished paper.
31   Barrows, op. cit., Chaps. 5–6.
32   John R. Cartwright, *Politics in Sierra Leone 1947–1967* (Toronto, 1970).
33   Quoted in ibid., p. 248.
34   Thomas S. Cox, *Civil–Military Relations in Sierra Leone. A Case Study of African Soldiers in Politics* (Cambridge, Mass., 1976), p. 18.
35   ibid., p. 60. Senior army officers were mostly Sierra Leoneans as a result of Africanization of key staff and command positions between 1964 and 1965.
36   Cox, op. cit., p. 74.
37   ibid., pp. 134–5.
38   Humphrey J. Fisher, 'Elections and Coups in Sierra Leone, 1967', *Journal of Modern African Studies*, 7, 4 (1969), pp. 611–36.
39   Cox, op. cit., p. 86.
40   ibid., pp. 136–7.
41   ibid., p. 212.
42   ibid., p. 213.
43   ibid., p. 217.
44   See Samuel Decalo, *Coups and Army Rule in Africa. Studies in Military Style* (New Haven, 1976) for this argument.
45   ibid., p. 27.
46   For examples of corruption under military regimes in Nigeria, see Dudley, op. cit., p. 81 and Reference Note No. 36 on pp. 317–19.
47   Nicole Ball, 'The Military in Politics: Who Benefits and How', *World Development*, 9, 6 (1981), pp. 576, 580.

3 State and Economy

Colonial state and economy

The colonial state in Africa was in the hands of a bureaucracy. Although subject to directives from the metropolitan state in Europe, the colonial civil service enjoyed a degree of local autonomy. Moreover, the colonial state generally maintained relative autonomy from the owning elements of the colonial economy – local settler capitalists and foreign owners of local industries and plantations as well as the imperial bourgeoisie as a whole. Nevertheless, the colonial state was primarily responsive to these various sections of capital; it was hardly responsive to the interests of the non-owning groups, composed predominantly of the indigenous African peoples. The colonial bureaucracy performed a variety of functions which were supportive of the needs of capital. Its prime concern was to provide the conditions for capitalist production to take place as well as to be profitable. Colonial civil servants were far from being the administrative servants of capital but they were obliged to look after and promote the interests of the owning groups.

The foreign owners of local industries and agricultural estates – such as mining and agricultural companies – were generally the dominant economic force within the colonial territories and the state bureaucracy was typically most responsive to their interests. But other groups, such as those of the settlers in local trade and commerce, were also quite successful at times in obtaining close consideration of their needs by the colonial government. The white-settler communities resident in various parts of Africa were able to exercise an important influence on state policy. They were represented in the colonial legislature and the various councils of state. Thus the dominance of capital in the economic sphere was perpetuated by the political sphere.[1]

During the colonial period, African countries were made both politically and economically subordinate to the interests of imperial capital and, to a lesser extent, settler and foreign capital. Local economies were subordinated to externally defined needs and there occurred a total reorganization of pre-colonial patterns of production to meet such needs.

49

The needs of international production demanded that the African colonies produce industrial raw materials, both agricultural products and metals and minerals. African economies were integrated into the world capitalist system as suppliers of those materials required for industries in the capitalist metropolises. Imperial, foreign, and settler capital invested in agriculture oriented towards export production, mining and, occasionally, light industries. Those areas within colonial territories which, for geographical and other reasons, did not contribute to the production of exportable raw materials, were relatively neglected.

When the colonial bureaucrats departed from Africa, they left behind highly distorted economies. Capital was mainly in the hands of settler and foreign owning groups. African economies were geared to the production and export of primary products. In agriculture, for example, resources had been predominantly allocated to industrial crops for export rather than to food production for domestic consumption. African countries lacked manufacturing and capital goods industries, serving instead as dumping grounds for the surplus of manufactured goods of the western industrial nations. They were, moreover, extremely dependent on trade with the metropole powers, and they were dependent on, or subordinate to, metropolitan suppliers of capital, technology, skills and markets. There were strong links between the primary producing sectors and overseas markets and suppliers; but there were few economic connections between the various domestic sectors, and the various economic regions within any particular colonial territory were very uneven in their level of development.

African economies were, in sum, underdeveloped; that is, they lacked an indigenously oriented process of accumulation of a self-expanding nature.[2] The indigenization of African economies was a key concern of the nationalists. But unlike the goal of political indigenization, which was grounded in the common notion of independent statehood, economic indigenization has had various meanings and, unlike political independence, has proved more elusive to achieve.

Post-colonial state and economy

On the attainment of political independence, the states of the new African countries were no longer components or appendages of an imperial administrative structure. At the same time, capital – imperial, foreign and settler – no longer enjoyed easy and direct access to the state apparatus. Although large segments of African economies were dominated by non-indigenous capital, this capital had limited involvement in the political process of African countries. The post-colonial state thus possessed some degree of autonomy from non-indigenous owning groups.

The stratum of society that internally assumed the power of the state after independence may be characterized in general terms as 'middle class'. Power did not pass into the hands of an indigenous bourgeoisie, since colonialism had generally prevented the emergence of a fully-fledged and economically viable bourgeoisie. The banks, plantations and larger industrial firms were predominantly foreign owned. There did exist in some countries a commercial bourgeoisie but that too was composed of persons drawn from alien settler communities (Asians, Europeans, Lebanese) to whom power could not be transferred. Moreover, since workers and peasants had not constituted a coherent challenging force during the period of nationalist struggle, power had also not fallen into their hands. It was clear, therefore, that some element of the African 'middle class' would take over state power at independence.

Many of the nationalist politicians that manned the post-colonial political institutions were from the petty-bourgeois class of small-scale capitalists such as shopkeepers, traders, family farmers and self-employed artisans. But there were other nationalists who assumed the power of the state who were drawn from another group – not a class – composed of civil servants, teachers, ministers of religion, and full-time politicians. As to which of these two elements of the 'middle class' inherited state power, this varied from country to country. In much of Africa it was a combination of petty producers and bureaucrats who took over control of the post-colonial state; but in some others the proportions varied. In Kenya, for instance, accession to state power was in the hands of an emergent indigenous bourgeoisie, while in countries such as Tanzania and Zambia, teachers and clerks were the mainstay of the independence movement.

In those countries where one section predominated, the element in the ascendency could have an important bearing on the nature of the post-colonial state, especially in regard to its economic orientation. As we shall suggest in our case-studies below, those drawn from a salariat have been more likely to favour the expanded role of the state sector in the economy, while those from the petty bourgeoisie have favoured the increasing role of private (especially African) enterprise. The character of African development strategies has depended in large part upon the complexion of the governing class, in particular whether its power base has derived from private wealth or bureaucratic position. In Kenya, the existence of an influential indigenous bourgeoisie at independence ensured that a private-capitalist strategy would be championed; while in Tanzania an ascendant bureaucratic stratum was to advocate the expanded role of the state. And, similarly, in the Ivory Coast (where a planter bourgeoisie controlled the PDCI and advocated private capitalism) and in Mali (where the Union Soudanaise was the emanation of bureaucrats advocating the development of an extensive public sector), the character of the class assuming state power determined, in important measure, economic strategy.[3]

Although the indigenous peoples now controlled the state apparatus, they had little ultimate control of the local 'capitalist-type' economy. Those with political power could exert relatively little economic power over the means of production in African countries: these were in the hands of non-indigenous capital. That political independence was not matched by economic independence was soon apparent to those who acceded to power. They widely acknowledged that political independence had no substance unless accompanied by economic independence. Thus the Nigerian second national development plan noted:

> Experience has shown that political independence without economic independence is but an empty shell and a truly independent nation cannot allow its objectives and priorities to be distorted or frustrated by the manipulation of powerful foreign investors.

Economic nationalism followed logically from political nationalism. President Nyerere of Tanzania has stated:

> Economic nationalism has nothing to do with the ideologies of socialism, capitalism, or communism. It is universal among nation states . . . Whatever economic system the people of different African countries eventually adopt, it is quite certain that sooner or later they will demand that the key positions of their economy are in the hands of their own citizens.[4]

Economic nationalism was the desire to secure greater indigenous ownership and national control of the economy.

But economic nationalism, as pursued in contemporary Africa, has manifested itself in two divergent modes of economic development. The first mode, as represented in most African countries and including ones such as Kenya, Nigeria and the Ivory Coast, entails the localization, or 'Africanization' of the economy, whereby the major means of production and distribution are gradually placed into the hands of the indigenous people. The basic features of the colonially inherited economy, however – the existence of private property and capitalist production – are preserved. This first mode of economic development emphasizes private capitalism and lays stress on the role of private enterprise although, in practice, state involvement in the economy is not unimportant. The second mode, of which we distinguish a number of variants, seeks in addition to the localization of the economy to modify or to abolish capitalism and to build socialism. In this second mode there is an attempt to transform – not maintain – the economic system derived from colonialism. The main instrument to restructure the national economy is the state. This second mode is represented in its less radical versions by countries such as Ghana under Nkrumah (1957–66), Mali (1960–8), Tanzania and Zambia, and in its more radical versions by Mozambique.

That the socialism of the former group of countries has been of a social–democratic variety and that of Mozambique of a Marxist nature is not surprising in view of the different character and evolution of the nationalist struggle. But in both sets of countries state involvement, based on socialist ideas rather than on private capitalism, has been a marked feature.

As to which of these two general modes of economic development a given African country undertakes is a complex question that has been answered in various ways. Our argument here is that the specific mode of development is determined to a large extent by, as indicated above, the political dispositions of the state personnel and also by the class forces which impinge on the state apparatus. The contribution of class pressures (both from local classes as well as those from external forces) in conjunction with the role of senior political leaders and government officials have shaped the economic policy of governments in post-colonial Africa.

The post-colonial state in Africa possesses a degree of autonomy relative to various classes, both domestic and external. The state is not the mere handmaiden of classes, especially the owning elements of the economy. In contemporary Africa local classes have been weak and have not wielded much influence on economic policy; their impact has not been absent but has generally been minimal. The state personnel – the leading politicians and civil servants – have therefore had an important influence in shaping policy; their orientations and dispositions, especially those of the top political leaders, have been of considerable weight. But in formulating policies state personnel have given consideration to the interest of non-indigenous capital as represented by its agents – the multi-national corporations and international aid agencies. The economic predominance of imperial, foreign and settler capital at the time of independence, although no longer manifested through direct political access to the state apparatus, has entailed constraints on policy-making. This is not to imply that the post-colonial state is a mere intermediary for foreign interests, but it has been obliged, by virtue of the extent of the financial, commercial and technological dependence of its economy on western capitalist countries, to be responsive to the foreign owning elements as well as the metropolitan bourgeoisie as a whole. Indeed, this responsiveness to foreign economic interests has been heightened in recent years, consequent upon Africa's worsening economic plight and her heavy dependence on foreign loans to sustain her economies.

In the sections that follow, we will be concerned with the impact of classes and state personnel on the form of economic development undertaken in a number of African countries. We will take Kenya and Nigeria as examples illustrating the private capitalist mode of economic development, and Zambia, Tanzania and Mozambique as representing various modes of development towards a form of socialism under the direction of the state.

But in addition to a consideration of the general form of economic development undertaken in certain African countries, we will be concerned with the actual nature of development that has ensued in particular economic sectors. Actual sectoral developments have also been affected by class forces and the orientations of state personnel and, particularly in our case-studies on Zambia and Tanzania, we will consider how concrete economic developments have been shaped by factors both internal and external to these African countries.

In sum, we are concerned with the politics of economic policy formulation and implementation as well as their relationship with the issue of economic independence.

In the previous chapter it was argued that the persons who have occupied the leading positions in the state system have used their power, *inter alia*, to advance their own economic interests. Political power has furthered a process of personal accumulation and enrichment. It is nonetheless not entirely adequate to explain the nature and role of African political and economic patterns in these terms alone. Such an approach places undue emphasis on the motivations of those who hold power, whilst underestimating the context in which the power-holders operate. In all African countries, great store has been laid on the achievement of economic growth and the raising of the living standards of the population. Economic development is the theme that has overridden all others. In the process of promoting economic development, it has been recognized that in all of these countries the state would play an important role, even in those countries laying stress on private enterprise. Many of those who have held power in Africa have been moved mainly by the desire to use the state for personal aggrandizement. But these personal motives could only be fulfilled if larger purposes were served as well. Those who have held state power have had to provide the conditions for production to take place and to be profitable. State personnel have thus also been concerned with national economic development. And in the process they have enhanced the possibilities to further their own appropriation. The state, in the name of economic development, has commanded quite considerable economic resources; their disbursement has provided ample opportunities for profit for state personnel.

Yet this concern with individual accumulation has been accompanied by another concern, the furtherance of group interests. As noted in the previous chapter, in order to attract allies and build a coalition supportive of the regime in power, governments have used their control over the allocation of public resources to favour the politically faithful. The selective apportionment of public resources (roads, water supplies, schools, clinics, loans, jobs and the like) has been an important means of organizing political support in most African countries. Those in control of state power have also used the state to promote the class interests of an emergent indigenous bourgeoisie with which they have been affiliated. In Kenya and Nigeria, for example, state personnel have had as their prime objective the strengthening of the economic position of indigenous capitalists. In Mozambique, Tanzania, and Zambia, on the other hand, control of the state has been used, to an important extent, to promote the corporate interests of the state personnel themselves. The deployment of quite considerable economic resources has created an economic base and a vested interest for those in command of the state.

We have noted above that the relative autonomy of the state enables state personnel to play a prominent role in shaping state economic policy according to their own dispositions. It is important therefore to recognize the interests that guide state personnel in their economic decision-making. No doubt they have been concerned with questions such as economic nationalism as well as national economic development and the promotion of the welfare of the mass of the people. But in important measure as well they have been concerned with their own individual interests and those of specific social classes (indigenous capitalists) and/or the state apparatus to which they have been affiliated. These various interests will be evident in the following discussion; but they are not pursued here in any detail. Our main concern is to consider the politics of state economic policy and the related issues of economic independence and foreign economic domination.

KENYA

The development strategy adopted by Kenya since independence in 1963 has been a capitalist one. An explicit statement of the strategy is to be found in Sessional Paper No. 10 (1965) on 'African Socialism in Kenya'. It entails the preservation of private property – of both indigenous and foreign capital – and also the support for the development of African capitalism and the promotion of foreign investment.

The development strategy was inspired by the class nature of the nationalist leaders who took over the reins of state power in 1963. The class that led the nationalist movement and gained control of the state apparatus at independence was a class of Kenyan capitalists. However modest and economically weak they may have been relative to foreign capital, they constituted an 'embryonic Kenyan bourgeoisie'. This class of African capitalists had developed particularly after the Second World War. It had been formed out of a salariat and had moved into small-scale agriculture and trade.[5] It was 'moderate' and firmly committed to the extension of indigenous capitalism. This embryonic bourgeoisie was to use state power to expand its operations and strengthen its economic base.

After independence the emergent domestic bourgeoisie proceeded to use state power to diminish settler (Asian and European) dominance of the economy, and to further its control over the means of production. The state was employed to facilitate the accumulation of this embryonic bourgeoisie. (At the same time radical elements within the ruling party, KANU, were purged.) The state was used to support African capitalist enterprise first in large-scale agriculture, then in commerce and more recently in manufacturing.

The first thrust of state support to indigenous capitalism was concerned with the transfer of land in the former 'white highlands' through settlement schemes. The prime agricultural land in the Rift Valley was taken over by a small number of African capitalists. The appropriation of land was to constitute a key source of surplus value to Kenyan capitalists.[6] The Kenyan capitalist class further used the state to enhance its control over the commercial sector of the economy.[7] The more powerful sections of the Kenyan bourgeoisie, due to their position within the state, tended to gain the most in the trading or service sectors. And in the 1970s control of the state by indigenous capital was used to establish a growing stake in manufacturing industry.[8] However modest this stake may still be, the indigenous capitalist class has begun to establish a place for itself in manufacturing. In connection with manufacturing industry, a related trend in the growth of indigenous capitalism has been the Africanization of management positions within foreign firms and the attempts by the state and private Kenyan capital to localize the ownership of foreign corporations. A high degree of Africanization of management positions took place in the 1970s; the state (especially in banking, oil-refining and cement-manufacture) and private enterprise (especially in tea-processing and shoemaking) have taken over control in many industrial sectors formerly dominated by foreign capital.[9]

Nevertheless, in spite of the use of the state to promote investment by the indigenous capitalist class in manufacturing, there has been continuing and increased penetration of foreign capital since independence in the Kenyan manufacturing sector. 'Industrial development has taken place since the late 1960s predominantly through the *partnership* form of joint ventures between state and/or local capital and foreign capital.'[10] In some instances foreign capital has been threatened because of competition by locally owned enterprises, whereas in other projects there has been collaboration between the local and foreign partners. But, as Swainson makes clear, 'where domestic and foreign capital compete, the state will invariably (as in the case of tea) act in support of national capital'.[11]

The overall picture has thus been one of expanding economic activity for the emergent domestic bourgeoisie. But the question that arises is whether, as in the case of Swaziland, this has been 'an expansion that is complementary to rather than conflicting with the interests of the foreign and settler bourgeoisies'.[12] It is clear that control of the state apparatus by the Kenyan middle class (composed of persons within the bureaucracy, politics, business and the professions) has been central to the advances made in the post-independence period and that this class has accumulated a substantial economic base in the private sector. But whether, as in Swaziland, the state in Kenya 'has acted in a way entirely consistent with the interests of the dominant class'[13] (that is, the foreign and settler bourgeoisies) by preserving and extending its position, or has served as a spring-board for the undermining of this position is a matter of considerable debate.

It is not possible to review this debate here.[14] But our own interpretation draws from both sides of the debate. One should, first of all, not overrate the extent of African industrial or productive activity. Most of the Kenyan middle class (petty bourgeoisie, emergent indigenous bourgeoisie, state personnel)

> remain for the most part speculators or parasites, not producers . . . They prefer to focus their attention on other enterprises with a quick effortless return. Thus, they accumulate through property speculation, through their control of parastatal bodies and marketing boards, through their political roles and positions within the civil service and administration, through the 'sleeping' partnerships they form with Asian businessmen, and – most importantly – through their involvement with foreign capitalists.[15]

In the second place, it is evident that the indigenization policies that have been pursued in Kenya since independence have not been directed so much at ending the domination of foreign capital (although they have been aimed at settler capital, both Asian and European) as ensuring that a small group of Kenyans develops a vested interest in it. 'African socialism' in Kenya has resulted in the growth of a small class of indigenous capitalists which is still dependent for its growth and accumulation on foreign capital. If this domestic capitalist class desires to expand further it will only be able to do so through connections with foreign financial and technical sources. Although there has taken place an increase in state and private Kenyan participation in the ownership of industrial enterprises, much of this has been conducted through the partnership form. Such partnership in the ownership of projects does not necessarily signify control and, especially in the case of the larger projects, most operate under management and technical consultancy contracts with foreign firms as well as rely on international finance. The position of foreign capital in the manufacturing sector has thus been largely maintained.

NIGERIA

During the colonial period there emerged in Nigeria an indigenous commercial bourgeoisie which overlapped with a small professional elite. In the 1950s, 'alliances of commercial, professional and bureaucratic classes, and in the North the office-holding aristocracy appropriated political power'. The transfer to Nigerians of control over the economy has been a basic plank of government policy since independence. The emergent indigenous bourgeoisie used state power 'to accumulate money, finance their political activities, appropriate commercial opportunities, [and] extend the areas of economic activity reserved to Nigerian businessmen'.[16]

Indigenization of the commercial sector of the economy proved slow. But with the launching of the second national development plan, 'in order to ensure that the economic destiny of Nigeria is determined by Nigerians themselves',[17] there was promulgated in February 1972 the Nigerian Enterprises Promotion ('Indigenization') Decree (NEPD). Its provisions required that a range of economic activities in the hands of non-nationals should be wholly taken over by Nigerians with the latter also holding a majority or minority owning in other economic concerns. The main purpose of the 1972 decree (and that of the revised one introduced in 1977) was thus to reserve certain economic activities exclusively for Nigerians while also enabling Nigerians to purchase shares in larger concerns. To facilitate the provisions of the decree, the government established a Nigerian Enterprises Promotion Board and a publicly funded bank for commerce and industry while also directing that commercial banks allocate at least 40 per cent of loans to Nigerian businesses. The Nigerians who purchased shares have been the already privileged ones – managers, civil servants, businessmen, military officers. Foreign companies have withdrawn from certain economic sectors such as commerce (although they are still important in the import and wholesale trade) and have moved into manufacturing. Indigenous investment is therefore predominant in the service, retailing and small-scale industrial sectors. Some indigenous entrepreneurs, however, have entered into partnership with the state or with foreign industrialists and Nigerian penetration of manufacturing is increasing. But this is still on a very dependent basis with foreign capital; most of the industrial production is dependent on foreign management, technology and imported inputs, and, indeed, the government continues to extend a warm welcome to foreign investors in this sector.

It is evident that all that the decrees have achieved – and all that they were very likely intended to achieve – is the promotion of indigenous capitalism. The Nigerian state has been primarily engaged in fostering a domestic bourgeoisie.[18] As in Kenya, the effect of state economic policy has been to convert state personnel – civilian politicians, military rulers, top bureaucrats – as well as their commercial allies into a new property-owning, rentier class. State personnel, in particular, have been able to acquire the necessary resources – through access to loans and credit or through 'kickbacks' from the award of contracts and licences – to purchase shares in on-going enterprises or enter into the commercial housing market and urban real estate.

The economy itself, however, has not undergone any restructuring and there has not been any basic structural change in the inherited set of economic institutions. The oil boom (Nigeria became sub-Saharan Africa's major exporter in the 1970s) has not introduced any fundamental changes in the nature of the economy except to make that economy even more underdeveloped and dependent on metropolitan capital. Indeed the massive earnings from oil-production have resulted in serious crises in the capitalist-type economy. Huge sums have been expended in the sphere of consumption – education, the military, prestige projects, road-construction and imports of consumer goods. The expansion of industry and infrastructure has been hindered and agriculture has been neglected, resulting in the collapse of agricultural exports and a rapid rise in food imports. As the oil boom has faded since the late 1970s, the seriousness of these crises has made Nigeria turn with mounting urgency to foreign loans to sustain its budget and also to multinational corporations and international aid agencies (the World Bank has moved into agriculture on a large scale). The position of foreign capital has been maintained and there is a continued domination of foreign enterprise in many sectors. In Nigeria an independent and autonomous domestic capitalist economic order has begun to be established but the economy as a whole still remains highly dependent on foreign capital.

In both Kenya and Nigeria, therefore, policies of indigenization have led to the development of an indigenous bourgeoisie while at the same time the dominant place of foreign capital has only been marginally affected. The thrust of indigenization has not been so much the elimination of 'neo-colonial' dependence as the establishment of a new accommodation with it. And the nature of the economy inherited from colonialism has remained virtually intact. Capitalist production relations and private property have been essentially preserved and perpetuated as have the distorted and underdeveloped character of economic life. What development has taken place has consolidated a lopsided economic structure whereby the interests of a group of African capitalists and state personnel have been enhanced.

ZAMBIA
Zambia at the time of independence in 1964 possessed the classic characteristics of the phenomenon of underdevelopment. There was an overwhelming dependence upon the copper-mining industry which provided the bulk of state revenues. Manufacturing and the service

sector were small while agriculture – apart from a tiny minority of European commercial farmers – had been grossly neglected. African education had also received little serious attention during the colonial period and there was an acute shortage of educated, skilled and trained manpower. And, finally, there was a paucity of indigenous control of key sectors of the economy with foreign firms and non-citizens owning and controlling most industry, commerce, financial institutions and commercial agriculture.

The colonial government had been dependent financially on foreign mining capital: the two major copper-mining companies were the key generators of local surplus from which the colonial government derived its administrative revenues. As a consequence, the colonial bureaucracy had been responsive to the needs of alien mining capital. Moreover, the influence of settler capital on policy had also been strong, especially in the 1930s and 1940s when white settlers held a majority of seats in the Legislative Council.

During the immediate post-colonial years, the new Zambian government did little to alter the inherited economic structure. No attempt was made to displace foreign or settler capital and, indeed, further foreign investment was specifically encouraged as promoting economic development. Private property and capitalist production continued to be affirmed. However, the new UNIP government did take steps to improve considerably the level of social welfare for the mass of the people. Because of the populist character of the Zambian nationalist movement, the regime which acquired state power devoted substantial funds to increasing the general welfare and quality of life of the common man. But otherwise the economic structure remained the same as before.

Within a few years of independence, however, important changes from the economic policy of the erstwhile colonial state began to take place. An important shift in government policy was exemplified in a series of so-called economic reforms in 1968, 1969, and 1970, whereby indigenous ownership and control were increased. On the one hand, certain sectors of the economy were reserved exclusively for Zambian citizens and, on the other hand, the state acquired a majority of shares in a number of former settler and foreign companies. Speaking in April 1968 on the occasion of the announcement of the first package of economic reforms, President Kaunda made it apparent that the structure of ownership, particularly in the commercial and industrial sectors of the economy, had to be changed. In the words of the president: 'time is now that we must take urgent and vigorous steps to put Zambian business firmly in the hands of the people themselves just as political power is in their hands'.[19] During this speech and in subsequent speeches in the next two years the president related measures his government would take to reserve certain spheres of economic activity exclusively to citizens. These areas – retail and wholesale trade, building-material industries, transportation – were to be removed from settler ownership and reserved only for indigenous private enterprise.

During the years 1968 to 1970 the president also announced that the state intended to take over various industries and firms in order to attain greater indigenous control of the economy. A number of mostly resident expatriate manufacturing companies was taken over by the government in these years, and in 1969 the giant copper-mining companies were placed under state control. The following year Kaunda publicized plans – which were only partially implemented – to absorb the commercial banks, insurance companies and building societies into the state sector. As elsewhere in Africa, these various economic reforms represented a deliberate attempt to commence the process of indigenization of the economy.

The economic reforms announced between 1968 and 1970 stemmed from class pressures as well as the general orientation of government leadership, as members of the indigenous petty bourgeoisie pressed for government assistance against settler capital. African petty traders and artisans appealed to the government to enact measures on their behalf to enable them to compete with settler capital just as the colonial government had provided state assistance to the settlers during colonial times.[20]

But the influence of these class pressures did not entail the sole, or even the main, determinants underlying governmental policy. Political leaders and government officials – the policy-makers – had ideological orientations which had a decisive effect on policy formation. The sources of these ideological dispositions were complex. In the first place political leaders gradually became aware of the contradiction between control of the polity and control of the economy. The former was in the hands of local politicians but the latter was in the hands of foreign and settler capitalists. The politicians could exercise only limited control over the economy and only tangentially influence local capitalist production. Secondly, the politicians gradually became aware of various practices adopted by members of the resident expatriate business community which were detrimental to the interests of national development. Such predatory practices as overcharging and over-invoicing were considered to be widespread and were severely condemned. The politicians were particularly concerned about the investment and development policies of the copper-mining companies. To eliminate illegal practices and promote the desired sort of development (as well as to indigenize control of the economy), the government began to favour the takeover or removal of certain economic activities from non-citizens.

In 1967 the president had introduced the doctrine of Humanism. This placed emphasis on the role of the state in the economy but also indicated that private enterprise would be acceptable in Zambia's 'mixed economy'. The mixed nature of the state's economic orientation was a reflection of the complexion of the leadership of the nationalist movement, composed of petty bureaucrats and a petty bourgeoisie. In spite of some of its anti-capitalist and egalitarian arguments, the government's economic reforms promoting economic nationalism were well-disposed towards capitalistic forms of production. Zambian politicians and government officials were not ideologically inclined to undermine capitalist production in Zambia. What they essentially desired was to place the economy in the hands of Africans. As a result they enacted measures to promote an African owning group to replace former settler capital while large-scale and more technologically complex industries were to be absorbed directly by the state. The economic reforms were, therefore, as many have claimed, anti-imperialist rather than anti-capitalist.

That the economic reforms would not undermine capitalist forms of production was well understood by foreign and metropolitan capital. As the dominant economic forces within the Zambian economy they could have been expected to oppose the government's measures to localize the economic structure. But because the reforms would not be incompatible with their interests they did not intervene. Nationalization was not viewed as necessarily antithetical to the interests of international capital. Indeed they welcomed government participation in their businesses.[21] The multinational corporations realized that the Zambian government could not afford to dispense with foreign expertise, and they could willingly surrender equity in their local assets in the knowledge that the joint ventures and/or management and technical agreements they negotiated would leave them with substantial control and a reasonable rate of return.

The economic reforms have led to the emergence of a small class of indigenous owners. Together with the much larger class of petty commodity producers (the petty bourgeoisie) they gradually grew in political prominence during the 1970s. Indigenous owners achieved a direct presence in Zambia's parliament and began to exert increasing influence on policy. The thrust of this pressure was to push the government into a less ambiguous capitalist orientation. The doctrine of Humanism proclaimed by the political leadership contained many conflicting principles. On the one hand it was hostile to the accumulation of property and to capitalist exploitation. Such egalitarian tendencies were reflected in the government pursuing policies such as the Leadership Code, to advance the interests of the common man. On the other hand, Humanism was not opposed to some degree of private enterprise and the government, as we have noted, pursued policies specifically related to fostering the growth of indigenous capital. The emergent indigenous owning group sought to overcome these contradictions by urging the government to set the economy more firmly on a strict capitalist course. Through their own organizations as well as through their parliamentary representatives they called into question the extent of state involvement desirable in the economy; proposed policies more accommodating of foreign capital and private investment; and advocated greater state assistance to indigenous business.[22]

And, indeed, indications are that pressure from indigenous capital contributed to another, albeit slight, shift in the direction of Zambia's development policies. A revised Industrial Development Act, passed in 1977, provided various incentives to attract foreign investment with the assurance that nationalization of property would only occur in certain specific circumstances. But the government did not transfer any parastatal firms to private hands. President Kaunda continued to warn against the consequences of exploitative capitalism and little further encouragement was given by the state to fostering a larger indigenous owning class. As he maintained since the 1968 reforms: 'We do not propose to make of Zambians business barons now or in the future.'[23]

State capital has remained the dominant form of capital within Zambia. The extension of direct participation by the state into various industries and firms was undertaken in order to attain greater indigenous control of the economy. It was also hoped that state enterprise would assist in easing the dependence on foreign capital as well as make production more oriented to social needs, rather than subject to considerations of profit. As the following case-study of public enterprise and industrial development shows, however, public ownership has done little to diminish dependence on foreign capital. Nor has it undermined capitalist production relations and become oriented to mass consumption needs. Zambian state capital has been unable to break out of the inherited economic framework.

In the field of manufacturing industry the Zambian government began from 1968 to acquire majority shareholding in the most important private industrial enterprises. Public ownership was instituted in order to diminish dependence on foreign capital. 'State participation,' according to an important party document, 'is designed to guarantee the control of the economy by the Zambian people [and] the reduction of the impact of foreign influence in shaping national destiny.'[24] It was also envisaged (as reflected in party and government documents and in national development plans) that state enterprise in manufacturing would promote industries which were import-substituting, export-oriented, and employment-generating, relying as far as possible on local resources. The stated aims also included the establishment of small-scale industries in the rural areas in order to provide more geographically balanced industrial development.[25] The Industrial Development Corporation of Zambia (Indeco) was assigned the task of giving direct and concrete expression to these aims in manufacturing.

Not only was Indeco unable to diminish dependence on foreign capital, but public ownership did not lead to the emergence of a structure of production in accordance with official party and government objectives. Much recent manufacturing development initiated by Indeco has been judged to have been largely capital-intensive, urban-based, and directed towards the production of consumer goods, a number of which are luxury items, requiring the importation of a considerable volume of raw materials and intermediate products.[26] Finally, Indeco has undertaken projects that are not always profitable. Indeed, in recent years the level of returns has been very low (around 2 per cent of total turnover) and in some years Indeco has made net losses (amounting to around 2 per cent of turnover). Why has Indeco not lived up to expectations?

Account has to be taken of the nature of the excessive dependence of Zambia's economy on foreign economic interests. The dimensions of dependence are various and include reliance on foreign markets, capital, technology and designs, and managerial talents. In all the takeovers of private companies and in all the new ventures entered into after 1968, the acceptance of a considerable degree of continued dependence was acknowledged by the retention of foreign administrative and technical management through contracts. Continuing dependence on foreign managerial and technical skills (as well as inflows of foreign capital) has had an important bearing on the pattern of manufacturing development. Because of the constraints on sufficiently trained and qualified indigenous manpower, Indeco was obliged to rely on foreign companies to provide advice, skilled personnel, and feasibility studies. There was also a reliance on foreign finance capital and machinery and equipment for carrying out investments. The result has been that many investment decisions as well as the structure of investments (including choice of techniques) were based on the existence of foreign companies willing to recommend and carry out a project.

Zambia's industrialization policy followed the classic import-substitution pattern. Import-substitution was especially applied to consumer foods which cater for the consumption habits of the Zambian middle class (47 per cent of the manufacturing contribution to Gross Domestic Product is supplied by the food, beverage and tobacco industries). The fact that these products aim to satisfy the high-quality demand of the higher income groups has led to the use of technologically complex production techniques, and Indeco has had to incorporate the technology (and management) of western industrialized countries. Evidence on individual projects indicates that Indeco set up various capital-intensive industries such as a car assembly plant and various grain-mills. Even in cases where alternative technologies were available, factories were installed that were dependent on highly capital-intensive technology from abroad Zambia Clay Industries, for example, set up two ultra-modern brick factories in 1975 despite the existence of a number of older, labour-intensive operations scattered throughout Zambia. The bias of investment in favour of capital-intensive production has also ensued because the overseas firms 'profit from the supply of equipment, components, and technical services which embody capital-intensive techniques'.[27] Profits are often highest in the building of a plant and supply and maintenance of machinery. In Zambia as well, foreign companies have through indirect means – such as the provision of finance and credit – been able to influence the adoption of capital-intensive techniques. In recent years just over 50 per cent of Indeco capital was raised on international finance markets and Indeco was thus heavily dependent on foreign finance. The availability of foreign credit for overseas projects which favour the use of foreign capital equipment has also been an important factor. President Kaunda made the following observation:

It has been our experience in the past that foreign economic assistance has the tendency to distort our choice of technology for it has been invariably tied to purchase of machinery and equipment, etc., in the respective donor country. This condition has resulted in the importation of machinery and equipment which have generated very little employment for the local people.[28]

A final problem that has to be noted stems from foreign companies, commissioned to provide plant, not carrying out their work properly with the result that technical deficiencies have afflicted Indeco companies. When the German contractors handed over the brick-making factory at Kalalushi to Indeco it was discovered that the machines did not have any spare parts; that the machinery installed was obsolete so that it could not be replaced or repaired; that the machines were unsuited to local types of coal, and that the cost of the machinery was exorbitant. A Japanese company was responsible for commissioning a factory to produce fertilizer for Nitrogen Chemicals. Technical problems, however, consequent upon failures of construction, led to the factory being shut down on various occasions, and to Indeco being paid compensation of nearly one million *kwacha*. In the case of machinery installed by the Finns at Mansa Batteries, a parliamentary committee commented that the machinery was

installed on an experimental basis since it had never been used elsewhere in the world including its country of origin . . . the key problem of machine failure to reach its estimated output arose from the fact that it was a prototype, i.e., it was the first of its kind to be made and used and its basic design was not intended for continuous operation for long periods.[29]

Taking into consideration the repayment of foreign loans for financing the plant, and the expenses of foreign management,[30] it is clear that dependence on foreign contractors and managers has its price.

But internal factors also affected Indeco's performance. In the first place the government's industrial development strategy was not of sufficient precision to provide Indeco with clear guidelines for its activities. Clearly defined and unambiguous criteria for investment and operating decisions were not officially enunciated. The result was that many of Indeco's investments were selected according to *ad hoc* criteria. In the absence of any overall strategy the assumption of government and parastatal officials was not different from those of the foreign associate. For both parties, decision-making tended to be dictated primarily by short-term opportunity and local demand considerations (for beer and cigarettes, or cars) rather than by the implementation of a self-reliant industrial strategy to restructure the economy. But by adopting the short-term profit criteria, Indeco preferred investments in import-substitution industries producing more or less luxury goods as well as large, capital-intensive projects in the urban centres.

Secondly, Indeco was subject to a series of *ad hoc* political directives on specific operational issues, including type and location of investments. Projects were undertaken on political decisions although, as in the case of Mansa Batteries, the feasibility study concluded that the project based in Mansa would be uneconomic. Moreover, projects such as the Chinese maize mill at Chingola were started without any feasibility study being conducted; the decision was a purely political one, which led to the already planned and evaluated maize mill in Kitwe being abandoned. Directives were also issued regarding the location of projects. The locations of Livingstone Motor Assemblers, Kapiri Glass Products and Mansa Batteries, all subsidiaries of Indeco, were decided on the basis of providing employment opportunities outside the major urban areas. These and similar projects ran into difficulties for various reasons, partly because being located in up-country centres they were situated a long way from the main markets. Multi-million-pound brick factories were set up under official directive in the rural areas at Kalalushi and Nega Nega, but transporting the bricks long distances to the construction sites raised the cost of the bricks to uneconomic levels, with the result that the construction industry increasingly switched to the use of concrete blocks. Because of declining demand for its products, the brick works at Nega Nega was forced to close down in 1979 and the factory at Kalalushi was making large losses.

The acute shortage of administrative and managerial expertise was a recurring problem in Indeco. But effective Zambian management was adversely affected by political involvement. The parastatals suffered an extremely high rate of transfers of middle and top management, stemming from conscious government decisions to move managers between companies, especially to avert corruption. Inevitably the result was loss of efficiency. Management was also seriously affected by the politically inspired appointments of many less than qualified managers. The ensuing mismanagement was accompanied by a growing degree of corruption. State officials increasingly used their positions within Indeco to benefit themselves, and co-operated with politicians to their mutual advantage.

The economic reforms initiated in 1968 which resulted in state ownership reflected strong nationalist sentiments. The state now has greater access to economic surplus and is able to retain profits which would otherwise have left Zambia. But state capital is having to accommodate a good deal to foreign capital. Public ownership has not succeeded in diminishing dependence on foreigners. More importantly, state ownership has not – owing to external dependence and domestic political factors – succeeded in achieving the government's economic objectives, at least in manufacturing industry. What has evolved over the past fifteen years has been a form of state capitalism with various joint state-private ventures which has accommodated the forces demanding less direct foreign control.

The economic reforms also resulted in the growth of the state bureaucracy. State participation in various sectors of the economy has grown enormously as has the number of parastatal organizations (of which there were 112 in 1978). State economic participation has been premised on the promotion of national economic interests as well as the needs of the mass of the people. But it has also created an economic base for those in control of state enterprise. State personnel have used their positions either to enrich themselves or to accumulate in order to establish themselves at a later date in private business and farming. Through their control of quite considerable economic resources they have been able to promote their own individual and corporate interests.[31] A private economic sector has been available alongside the development of state capitalism, and this has been to the advantage of those state personnel wishing to transfer to private enterprise. Yet, unlike the situation in Kenya and Nigeria, the state has done little to foster the growth of indigenous capitalism. Instead it has permitted state personnel to use the state apparatus to promote their own interests with a number then branching out into the private sector.

State capital remained the dominant form of capital in Zambia. But it was not concerned with the wholesale transformation of the economic order. The state bureaucracy – parastatal officials and civil servants – steeped in conservative values and outlooks were not concerned about economic structural transformation. Despite the rhetoric of Humanism, strong political direction towards a socialist order was also not forthcoming. Together with foreign capital, state personnel continue to have a defining influence over the activities of state enterprises which do little to change the underdeveloped, distorted, and capitalist economic system inherited from colonialism.

TANZANIA

As in Zambia, the immediate post-colonial years in Tanzania saw a continuation of the economic structure inherited from colonialism. The new Tanzanian leaders envisaged development being achieved through further foreign investment as well as continuing production of raw materials (coffee, cotton, sisal, tea) for export. But as in Zambia, a decisive shift took place in government policy with the publication of the Arusha Declaration in 1967.[32] Since then Tanzania, under its new policy of 'socialism and self-reliance', has adopted a novel package of policies to restructure the country's inherited economy and to cut the links of dependency with the international capitalist system. Tanzania's strategy of socialist development first emphasized state ownership of the major means of production. Nationalization was resorted to in order to control those sectors of the economy – trading, financial, and industrial – under foreign ownership with a view to retaining surpluses at home as well as realizing the goals of structural transformation. Another policy adopted was the attempt to achieve collectivization in the rural areas – the *ujamaa* villages programme. In Tanzania, in fact, collective rather than individual interests have been stressed. This has led to the co-operatives in agriculture and the trading sector, and various areas of private profit have been closed off to entrepreneurially inclined Tanzanians.

At the time of independence in 1961, all local classes were too weak to wield much direct influence over the new state in its economic policy formation. Although it has been argued that the workers exerted pressure and pushed the government into the Arusha Declaration,[33] there is little evidence to support this assertion; and, likewise, the impact of the petty bourgeoisie (traders and farmers) and the peasants over governmental policy was minimal. It was the governing group – composed of the leading politicans and civil servants – which determined the specific form of economic development that Tanzania undertook. But although these state personnel enjoyed a high level of autonomy relative to all the other classes, they were subject to the influence of metropolitan capital, by whom their policies were often favourably viewed. Foreign capital was, for example, fully compensated where industry was nationalized and various economic links were maintained with western companies.

The nationalist leadership that inherited state power was drawn largely from bureaucratic elements (clerks, teachers) within the African middle class. The rest of the middle class, especially the petty bourgeoisie, was very weak. The class origins of the political leadership may possibly have had some influence on the economic policies of the TANU government after 1967. But the nature of the development strategy advocated by Tanzanian state personnel has various explanations: the populist nature of the nationalist movement (entailing the promotion of the interests of the masses); the anti-capitalist and social democratic leanings of President Nyerere;[34] and the experiences of immediate post-colonial developments (especially economic problems resulting from falling prices of Tanzania's key exports; lack of direct foreign investments; and continuing domination by foreign and settler capital of the major sectors of the economy).[35]

Yet, in spite of socialist proclamations, the process of socialist construction in Tanzania has remained a difficult and elusive objective. Tanzanian socialism, despite some signal achievements, has not been successful in establishing a basis for autonomous development. As in the case of Zambia, the nationalizations have not entailed full socialization,[36] and there is continuing dependence on and penetration of foreign capital and management. More importantly, Tanzania ran into an enormous economic crisis in recent years, consequent upon various external factors such as the $250m expense incurred following the collapse of the East African Community in 1978 and the $500m paid out as a result of the intervention of Tanzanian troops in the liberation of neighbouring Uganda; but also due to a variety of internal factors such as parastatal mismanagement and corruption. Tanzania's economy is kept afloat through some $695m of foreign aid per year – making it Africa's biggest recipient of western aid – and such aid supports at least 60 per cent of its annual development budget. The absolute amount of foreign borrowing, a decade after the Arusha Declaration, was more than twenty-one times greater than in 1967, and has called into doubt Tanzania's objectives of socialism and self-reliance.[37]

The governing group has been unable to transform Tanzanian society fundamentally. It has been argued that this is because the 'ideological bent of much of the elite' is still suspicious of 'mass line politics and the democratising logic of protracted struggle in the economic sphere'.[38] The conservatism of state personnel is not to be underestimated; Tanzanian leadership has been reformist and cautious. There has also been a struggle among the various tendencies within the governing group. The 'progressive' faction has been in the ascendancy much of the time and its members have advocated more socialist directions to development policy. But they have possessed a marked social-democratic ideology, rejecting the idea that socialism in Tanzania must come through the struggle of conflicting classes. They have argued that socialism could arise apart from the class struggle and progress would occur without drastic change; the transition to socialism would be via the peaceful road. However, of even greater importance is the fact that of large sections of the state personnel, especially those in the main bureaucratic decision-making bodies, it 'can hardly be said that [they] have fully and actively engaged themselves in the task of socialist construction'.[39] The state bureaucracy – high-level civil servants, parastatal officials, and party leaders – are opposed to a revolutionary ideology and radical socialist struggle. In other words there are objective constraints in an under-developed country like Tanzania seeking structural transformation. In a situation where there is no large working class and the peasantry is not radicalized, any transformation lies in the hands of the bureaucratic elite. As we shall see, the bureaucracy has been in a key position, to have a defining influence over the socialist initiatives promulgated by the party's leadership.

If there is a single touchstone of Tanzania's socialist project, it is the programme for the establishment of *ujamaa* villages in the rural areas of Tanzania where more than 90 per cent of the population lives. Rural development through a broad-based mobilization of the people (rather than through the previous capital-intensive settlement schemes) was perceived as a means of economic advancement not dependent on foreign capital as well as a social undermining of the trend towards the development of a class system in the rural areas.

In September 1967 President Nyerere issued a policy paper entitled 'Socialism and rural development',[40] in which he proposed the creation of *ujamaa* villages. These would be collective villages which would boost agricultural production, instil a spirit of collective life and work among the people, and improve the material conditions of the rural population. Nyerere described the *ujamaa* villages as 'rural *economic and social communities where people live together for the good of all*, and which are interlocked so that all of the different communities also work together in co-operation for the common good of the nation as a whole'.[41] There was to be a gradual transformation of rural life from small, scattered family plots towards co-operative living and work in *ujamaa* villages. The collective villages were to be implemented politically through education and mass political mobilization of peasants. Nyerere also made it clear that participation in *ujamaa* villages would be voluntary and that they could not be established by compulsion. The collective villages were to be implemented democratically by the rural people and largely through their own resources.

But this policy of 'persuading' the peasantry to move voluntarily into new villages and to take up communal farming was difficult to realize. Indeed as early as 1969 the government had begun to resort to both coercion and material inducements (provision of various social services, equipment and amenities) to induce peasants to resettle on their own. The introduction of 'operations' which combined both incentives and force to bring peasants in given areas into villages began. Between 1970 and 1973 various 'operations' were undertaken by the government to move all the people living in an area into 'planned' villages, usually with 250 or more families. Nyerere had argued that *ujamaa* living would have to start with small groups of people rather than, as was now the case in practice, with large populations. In spite of the provision at great cost of various social services and amenities and despite strenuous efforts by government and party officials, the pace of villagization proved extremely slow. Only two million peasants (about 15 per cent of Tanzania's total population) were living in *ujamaa* villages by 1973. In that year, however, the policy was extended to cover the whole country. Nyerere proclaimed in 1973 that 'to live in villages is an order', and TANU decided that the whole population should live in villages by the end of 1976. And by the end of 1976 thirteen million people lived in 7684 villages – renamed development villages – the result of forced massive resettlement.[42] It had been achieved at a cost. At times the forced movement of peasants entailed the burning or bulldozing of their houses; sometimes no importance was attached to the agricultural potential of the area or the availability of water. Both food and cash-crop production were affected.

According to the initial conception of *ujamaa* it was intended to establish democratically controlled and planned producer co-operatives organized and run by the peasants themselves. It was also intended that they be implemented politically through education and the political mobilization of peasants. But in the absence of sufficient numbers of political cadres, administrators and field staff were entrusted with planning and stimulating socialist production among the peasants. The *ujamaa* villages came to be controlled from 'above' through administrative action.[43] The implementation of *ujamaa* through government administration resulted in its redefinition. There was, first, the use of a large amount of force, or the threat of force, especially during the post-1973 period, when peasant enthusiasm was not much in evidence. Secondly, there occurred a removal of emphasis on the co-operative and democratic aspects and the placing of stress on villagization. Within the villages member involvement was extremely limited and decision-making remained in the hands of government officials.

So the policy of *ujamaa* villages turned out to be different in practice from what was intended in theory. This has been explained in various ways[44] but mainly as a consequence of the bureaucracy determining the whole outcome of development, including rural development in Tanzania. The bureaucrats have sought to control peasant production for two reasons. First, by controlling all the means of production in the country they are able to influence the nature and direction of development.[45] The peasants, just like those living in the urban areas, are an important section of the economy which the bureaucrats must attempt to control in order to extract a surplus of food to feed the cities and export crops to earn the foreign exchange to maintain or expand the state. The chief rationale of the villagization policy would thus appear to have been to concentrate the peasantry in administratively accessible units designed to raise the productivity of labour in household agriculture. By 1974 agriculture in Tanzania was stagnating with serious consequences for the financial basis of the state. Agricultural commodities constituted around half of Tanzania's GDP and virtually all her exports; their stagnation had to be overcome, the more so to support a burgeoning state bureaucracy and insure its reproduction. A second reason for control lies in the values with which the governmental bureaucracy has been steeped: those of direction and supervision. The technico-rational model that Mushi has seen as characterizing the behaviour of government officials has been opposed to the democratic decision-making and participation originally called for in the implementation of *ujamaa*. What was intended to be a self-managed project has turned out to be run by outsiders.[46]

As a result of serious productivity problems, mainly due to droughts (1973–4 and 1979–80) and low producer prices, Tanzania has in recent years become highly dependent on foreign aid donors, particularly the World Bank and American agro-business corporations, to boost agricultural production. But the World Bank and other donors are often biased towards agricultural export production and have favoured individual farmers rather than communal farmers.[47] Many of the large-scale farms that have been set up by foreign countries are also capital-intensive and capitalistic in organization. Moreover, external capital has also begun to enter into food-production and food-processing industries. The Tanzanian National Maize Project, adopted and started in 1976/7 at the behest of the World Bank, provides one such example. The net result of this dependence on foreign aid and inputs of foreign capital has been to perpetuate Tanzania's export-oriented economy and to call into question the twin goals of socialism and self-reliance.[48]

The main result of the Arusha Declaration was the growth and expansion of the governmental bureaucracy and the acquisition by state officials of control over the production process. The state bureaucracy became the custodian of state capital. State control of the economy was used, in part, to further the interests of incumbents of state office. Resources were expropriated – through taxes and price controls – from the peasants and rural producers to finance the salaries and privileges for a rapidly swelling state bureaucracy (which almost doubled in the 1970s). That part of the surplus derived from production which has been invested also suffered from parastatal corruption and mismanagement. (The National Milling Corporation, the major marketing parastatal for food-crops, incurred debts of over Shs 2 billion during the 1970s and was especially mismanaged.) Indeed parastatals and government enterprises served as vehicles of accumulation for politicians and government officials who were not permitted to accumulate in the private economic sphere. Ergas concludes that the parastatal system was 'primarily responsible for the country's enormous economic diffculties' and that their 'primary raison d'être now appears to be to serve the interests of the upper strata of the bureaucracy'.[49] State personnel used state power to advance their own individual and collective interests as against those of all other classes.

In both the Tanzanian and Zambian cases it is evident that appearance belied reality. Despite the rhetoric of socialism neither country assumed a revolutionary character. To be sure important economic changes were brought about: in particular, substantial nationalization occurred. But such government takeovers as well as expanding state participation in various sectors of the economy did not constitute the base for further moves towards the wholesale transformation of the economic order. A considerable degree of 'moderation' and 'responsibility' informed the actions of state personnel in Tanzania and Zambia and although these actions at times caused concern to foreign capital they did not, in reality, threaten drastically the interests of international capital, and in fact entailed some advantage to them. Indeed, state capital was closely linked with, and dependent on, foreign capital. State intervention in economic life has not fundamentally changed prevailing economic structures but has evolved into a form of state capitalism. Capitalist forms of production were preserved as were capitalist social relations of production. This is much more the case in Zambia where private enterprise was also preserved, although it has also not been entirely absent in Tanzania. Moreover, in both countries state capital has provided opportunities for private accumulation and the consolidation of the corporate interests of state personnel in opposition to all other classes. Those in control of the state apparatus, in the name of the development of a national economy, sought to curb foreign economic control and promote the welfare of the masses; and in both spheres some success was achieved. But at the same time they were not averse to advancing their own interests by using the state as an instrument of accumulation for themselves as a class.

Moreover, both countries ran into serious economic difficulties in recent years. Tanzania's economic crises have already been alluded to. In Zambia, a slump in copper prices and copper sales coupled with inflated import prices (especially of oil) as well as domestic mismanagement and misdirections of development priorities left the country with massive balance of payments deficits. Growing debt burdens forced both countries to turn to the International Monetary Fund for assistance and World Bank loans also increased. Economic dependence on foreign countries and institutions has thus been only marginally affected and Tanzania and Zambia's client status suggests that little transformation from the economies inherited from colonialism will be forthcoming.

MOZAMBIQUE

At independence in 1975 Mozambique's new rulers were bequeathed an economy underdeveloped and distorted by four centuries of Portuguese colonialism. In many respects, however, Mozambique inherited an economy similar to that which the other colonial territories possessed at the time of their independence. Its agriculture was export-oriented and dominated by large foreign plantations and settlers; African peasants were largely subsistence producers. Industrial development was limited and was also not related to the consumption needs of the mass of the people but oriented instead to those of the settlers and tourists. And, finally, there were strong economic ties with South Africa. Mozambique at independence was an underdeveloped and, consequent upon a bitter armed struggle for liberation, a war-ravaged land.

At independence the ruling party, Frelimo (Frente da Libertação de Moçambique), pledged itself to overcome economic underdevelopment. 'To win this war', stated President Samora Machel, 'we must fully and consciously assume the values that we gained during the national liberation struggle'.[50] Between 1964 and 1974, Frelimo had undergone certain experiences, which were to serve as an inspiration and as a guide for post-independence Mozambican society and life. During the protracted liberation struggle there had been established liberated zones (mainly in the north) in which political control had passed largely out of the hands of the Portuguese colonial administration and into those of Frelimo. In these zones, Frelimo proceeded to lay the foundations for new forms of economic production, social services, and political administration. It was here that the values gained during the liberation struggle were developed. Problems arose about the way to tackle development in the liberated zones. Should development serve the interests of the mass of the people, or would Frelimo simply replace the Portuguese colonial state? The decision was made in favour of the former. The crucial values which emerged during this period were the close association with the people in every situation; the principle of self-reliance; and the priority of politics over technical solutions. These values became the basic principles for development under the new conditions after independence.[51]

It is argued that those African countries, such as Mozambique, which attained independence through armed struggle are very different from those other countries in Africa which achieved their political independence constitutionally. The experiences of armed liberation struggle, including the administration and development of national liberated zones, are said to be such that the development of neo-colonial forms of nationalism become 'increasingly unthinkable' and lead instead to the construction of socialism.[52] But there are two problems with this argument which have had an important bearing on post-colonial developments in Mozambique. One is that three-quarters of the country was hardly touched by the liberation struggle. Another is that in Mozambique, as elsewhere in Africa, the leadership of the nationalist movement which took over state power at the time of independence was drawn from the petty bourgeoisie and professional groups. Saul and others suggest that a growing section of this middle class underwent a transformation during the armed struggle and, at independence, constituted the vanguard of the interests of the workers and peasants. But to what extent this is so is questionable,[53] as certain post-independence developments have revealed. Moreover, there is no certainty that a country which achieves independence through an armed liberation struggle will progress automatically towards the building of a socialist order.

Nevertheless, Frelimo has drawn 'on the rich experience of the liberated zones during the armed struggle' for framing its post-colonial economic policies. In particular, this is the case with the commitment to scientific socialism which Frelimo saw as being 'the affirmation of a process which was lived within the Mozambique Liberation Front, a rich, long and bitter process of class struggle'. For Frelimo 'Marxism–Leninism was not something we chose out of a book. It was in the process of the struggle that the people's interests asserted themselves and became more and more clearly demarcated from the interests of the colonialist exploiter and would-be national exploiter'.[54] 'Ideas came from practices', President Machel has observed; 'we evolved a theory out of our practice; and then we found that this theory of ours, evolving out of our practice, had already acquired a theorization under different circumstances, elsewhere, in different times and places. This theory and theorization is Marxism-Leninism.'[55]

After independence Frelimo committed itself to scientific socialism. At its third Congress in February 1977, it adopted scientific socialism as its ideology and proclaimed its intention to combine 'the revolutionary experiences of the Mozambican people with the universal principles of Marxism–Leninism'. The socialist revolution would take time to occur and entailed the 'intensification of class struggle', the creation of a 'New Man', and the development of the economy under state control. The class struggle was both an external battle against imperialism as well as an internal one to prevent the formation and growth of an exploiting stratum. The creation of a 'New Man' would reject both the pre-colonial and colonial tradition and mentality and would emerge out of the restructured economic and social order as one committed to socialism. The main instrument to implement the restructuring of the national economy would be the state. The state was to control, plan and direct all the main sectors of the economy and be dominant in economic production.

We have noted Frelimo's claim that the party's ideology was a synthesis of 'the revolutionary experience of the Mozambican people and the universal principles of Marxism–Leninism'. But it has proved difficult to reconcile the wartime experiences of Frelimo to the universal principles of Marxism–Leninism. As the Ottaways have argued:

it became increasingly clear that there was an underlying tension between Frelimo's new ideological commitment and its wartime experience. In fact, the history of Mozambique since the Congress has been to a large extent that of the conflict between the more centralizing tendency deriving from a

Soviet-type interpretation of Marxism–Leninism and the more decentralized and direct participatory tradition deriving from Frelimo's wartime experience.[56]

This tension was manifested most clearly in the area of rural development. Co-operative agriculture, *aldeias communais*, was practised in the liberated zones and was, after independence, declared to constitute 'the backbone of Mozambique's rural development strategy'. The establishment of communal villages was a task which 'must be fulfilled on the basis of the active participation of the population mobilized by, and integrated into the structures of the party'. The villages would be built through the villagers' own efforts and in the spirit of self-reliance. Yet in spite of this commitment to the communal village, co-operative agriculture received little government assistance, while more substantial amounts of government funds went into the new state farms. Indeed, priority was given to the state-farm sector which has been growing markedly since independence (partly as a consequence of state takeovers of abandoned settler farms and plantations as well as various colonial agricultural projects). This discrepancy between rhetoric and reality has been explained as the consequence of Frelimo's commitment to Marxism–Leninism and thus to a centrally planned economy (as well as being attributed to other factors such as the economic problems, especially in the agricultural sector, that the country faced immediately after independence). The concept of a planned economy conflicted with the idea behind the communal village. The latter was small, decentralized and largely autonomous, and was thus sharply at variance with the former.

In 1978 the Minister of Agriculture was dismissed partly for having disregarded the 'popular line', which advocated the setting up of communal villages, 'thus jeopardising one of our decisive development choices'. This brought to the fore a vital contradiction – that between man and machines (techniques). 'Systematically giving priority to technology, he scorned the people's initiative and contribution.'[57] During the liberation struggle priority had been given to man and political work over equipment and technical solutions. After independence there was a reversal of the priority. 'In essence, he does not place trust in the people, he does not consider man as the determining element of development.'[58]

The dismissal of the Minister of Agriculture was seen as a victory for the supporters of the more democratic and decentralized concept of the communal villages as against those advocating the more centralized and bureaucratic solution of state farms. Yet no fundamental shift has taken place in rural development strategy since 1978; the bias in government policy has persisted in favour of state farms. And the state-farm sector has, for its part, become extremely centralized. The formation of communal villages has proceeded faster in the north (the areas liberated long before independence), while elsewhere communal farming has been slow and individual production has continued to be dominant. By 1980, just over a thousand communal villages had been set up, grouping 1.5m peasants, or about 15 per cent of the total population. Out of these villages only about four hundred had some form of collective production. A strong statist tendency is becoming pronounced in Mozambique. The conditions prevailing at the time of independence encouraged such a development. With the sudden mass exodus of the larger part of more than 200 000 white settlers, and the abandonment of farms and factories, the state was forced to step in. And given the acute scarcity of trained Mozambicans to run these enterprises, the state was obliged immediately to take a preponderant role in their management. It is difficult as yet to reach any firm conclusions about the precise meaning of Marxism–Leninism in Mozambique. But the tendency towards a centrally planned economy based on the Soviet hierarchical model, is becoming more pervasive.

The state sector, however, has experienced a number of setbacks and difficulties. State personnel have either been relatively untrained Frelimo cadres catapulted into office in 1975, or opportunistic former Portuguese colonial officials able to retain their positions, since Frelimo simply took over the state structures created by the colonialists without reorganizing or transforming them. Mismanagement and corruption had a damaging effect on the performance of the state sector. In addition, a variety of external factors (such as higher oil prices, worsening terms of trade, natural disasters including floods [1977 and 1978] and drought, [1981–4], Rhodesian raids, and South African support of the armed terrorist Mozambique National Resistance Movement) have had a devastating impact on the Mozambican economy. Since 1980 Frelimo has attempted to re-orient its economic policy by co-operating with capitalism without compromising its commitment to the ultimate goal of a socialist society. Frelimo has sought to encourage small-scale private entrepreneurs – especially trying to persuade Portuguese exiles to return – as Mozambique needs middle-level expertise; and it has also invited foreign capital from the West to finance the development projects envisaged in the 10-year plan launched in 1980. But alongside this pragmatic co-operation, there have been continuing nationalizations and attempts to create a more centralized system of planning and organizing production. And private entrepreneurs and foreign capital have by no means been granted a free hand; they have to serve the national interest as well as be controlled in a planned socialist economy. As yet the opening up of the country to capitalist possibilities has not had much effect; little western investment has been forthcoming and few private traders have returned. Instead Mozambique announced in 1981 that it hoped to encourage investment from the USSR and eastern Europe and move along the road towards membership of the Soviet bloc economic organization Comecon (the Council for Mutual Economic Assistance).

To build socialism in Mozambique, Frelimo has opted for central planning of its economy and has become obliged to develop close economic ties with the Soviet-controlled Communist world.[59]

African economies and international capital

We have seen that a local bourgeoisie emerged within the new African states. This national bourgeoisie – either a bureaucratic one as in Tanzania, Zambia and Mozambique, or a private one as in Kenya and Nigeria – accumulates some surplus and has entered into agriculture, commerce and industry. The questions that arise are: what is the relationship between the national bourgoisie and international capital? To what extent is the local bourgeoisie independent from the international bourgeoisie? What is the extent to which the local bourgeoisie has acquired control over the surplus generated from local production so that it can influence its allocation into the various sectors of production?

Our case-studies have sought to show that although the local bourgeoisie acquired a greater measure of participation in the economy, it cannot be said that it constitutes an independent national bourgeoisie. The history of the national bourgeoisie has been one of conflict as well as coalition with international capital. The two parties have been united in their common desire to accumulate, and divided as a consequence of the national bourgeoisie's desire to achieve some degree of independence from international capital. The struggle between the two has resulted in new forms of co-operation, which, although allowing for greater participation by the national bourgeoisie, have still maintained the economic hegemony of international capital. Multinational corporations, for example, maintain their control, often through patent rights, over technology, monopoly over marketing and processing, and management and loan agreements, even where the enterprise is fully owned by nationals – whether with local private capital or state capital. Even in the area of agricultural production, although nationals have increasingly exerted control as in Kenya, international capital (in the form, for example, of the World Bank) has penetrated into the production process itself of various agricultural commodities. The national bourgeoisie has not yet managed to secure full control over the means of production or over the surplus; nor can it make decisions as to the utilization of investible surpluses.

The monopoly bourgeoisies in the advanced capitalist countries not only established total control over their national markets, but a section of the bourgeoisie turned international through export of capital. Capital has, during the present century, become internationalized. Today it is the capital of the 'international oligarchy', the monopoly corporations, which controls, directly or indirectly, production in the world capitalist economy. There has taken place a concentration of capital in the hands of monopolies on a global scale. The national economies of Africa have been penetrated by, and integrated into, the world capitalist economy. In every country subject to the rule of capital, capital rules, at the political level. In African countries, the state is run on behalf of the foreign bourgeoisie; it is the state of international capital.[60] Freyhold says of Tanzania that it is the metropolitan bourgeoisie 'which determines the core functions of the state and the actual dynamics of the economy'.[61]

However, this tends to overestimate the dominance of international capital. Post-colonial states in Africa enjoy a degree of relative autonomy from the direct control of the metropolitan bourgeoisie, who do not constitute a homogeneous and united class but one in which there is competition between rival monopolies. This relative autonomy explains why, at times, African states take actions independently of the international bourgeoisie. In regard to Kenya, Langdon writes of the existence of close ties between the state and multi-national corporations and shows that the Kenyan state has not been totally dependent:

> The many regulatory instruments the Kenyan state can use, its other sources of resources (such as foreign aid), and the influence on it of the emerging African bourgeoisie all mean that the state has some independence vis-à-vis the MNC sector, and can insist on a growing African share in the MNC privileges. The MNC sector, in turn, has an interest in close, co-operative relations with the Kenyan state, because of the many ways in which that state can provide subsidiaries with advantages in the local economy.[62]

Nevertheless, it is clear that actions taken by African states, and in particular the various 'indigenization' measures since independence, have not generally undermined the material power of international capital. The extent of manoeuvrability within the confines of world capitalist hegemony has its limits and African states have been unable to emancipate themselves from foreign economic domination. The chief results of 'indigenization' or economic nationalism in Africa have been to strengthen the economic bases of state and private capital, but without achieving effective control of national development. In countries such as Kenya and Nigeria domestic private capitalism has been supported by international capital, while in countries such as Tanzania and Zambia state capitalism has been financed and assisted by foreign capital. In a country such as Mozambique, a state bureaucratic system professing a socialist economic direction has sought to pose more of a challenge rather than just accommodate to internationalism; but with the exodus of most of its settlers and the limited extent of foreign penetration of its economy such a challenge has not amounted to much. Instead, by being obliged to make its development more dependent on the Soviet-controlled Communist bloc, Mozambique may discover limits to its economic actions from a non-capitalist source.

NOTES

1 For a discussion of the relations between the colonial state and classes in Kenya, see Nicola Swainson, *The Development of Corporate Capitalism in Kenya 1918-77* (London, 1980), pp. 1-12.

2 For a characterization of the structural features of dependence and underdevelopment, see Samir Amin, *Accumulation on a World Scale* (New York, 1974), pp. 15-20.

3 See, for example, Guy Martin, 'Socialism, Economic Development and Planning in Mali, 1960-68, *Canadian Journal of African Studies*, 10, 1 (1976), pp. 41-6 for Mali; and Bonnie Campbell, 'The Ivory Coast', in John Dunn (ed.), *West African States: Failure and Promise* (Cambridge, 1978), pp. 66-116. For Kenya and Tanzania see below.

4 *Second National Development Plan, 1970-1974* (Lagos, 1970), pp. 288-9; and Julius K. Nyerere, *Freedom and Socialism: A Selection from Writings and Speeches 1965-1967* (Dar es Salaam, 1968), p. 263.

5 For the growth of this class, see Swainson, op. cit., pp. 173-82.

6 For details of the use of state powers in regard to agrarian accumulation, see Colin Leys, *Underdevelopment in Kenya. The Political Economy of Neo-Colonialism* (London, 1975), Chap. 3.

7 For details, see Leys, op. cit., Chap. 5, and Swainson, op. cit., pp. 182-211.

8 For details see Colin Leys, 'Capital Accumulation, Class Formation and Dependency. The significance of the Kenyan Case', in Ralph Miliband and John Saville (eds.), *The Socialist Register 1978* (London, 1978), pp. 241-66.

9 See Leys, op. cit., Chap. 4, and Swainson, op. cit., pp. 212-35 for differing perspectives.

10 Swainson, op. cit., p. 17.

11 ibid., p. 18.

12 Isobel Winter, 'The Post-Colonial State and the Forces and Relations of Production: Swaziland', *Review of African Political Economy*, No. 9 (1978), p. 42.

13 ibid., p. 43.

14 See, for example, Rafael Kaplinsky, 'Capitalist Accumulation in the Periphery - The Kenyan Case Re-examined', and Colin Leys, 'Kenya: What Does "Dependency" Explain?', both in *Review of African Political Economy*, No. 17 (1980), pp. 83-105, 108-13. See also Björn Beckman, Imperialism and Capitalist Transformation: Critique of a Kenyan Debate', *Review of African Political Economy*, No. 19 (1980), pp. 48-62.

15 For a recent summary discussion of capitalist development (and exploitation) in Kenya, see 'Looters, Bankrupts and the Begging Bowl: Our Plundered Economy', *Race and Class*, 24, 3 (1983), pp. 267-86. The quotation is from p. 271.

16 See Gavin Williams, 'Editorial', *Review of African Political Economy*, No. 13 (1978), p. 2.

17 *Second National Development Plan*, op. cit., p. 289.

18 See, for example, Paul Collins, 'Public Policy and the Development of Indigenous Capitalism: The Nigerian Experience', *Journal of Commonwealth and Comparative Politics*, 15, 2 (1977), pp. 127-50; and Björn Beckman, 'Whose State? State and Capitalist Development in Nigeria', *Review of*

African Political Economy, No. 23 (1982), pp. 37–51.

19   K. D. Kaunda, 'Zambia's Economic Revolution', p. 27. An address to the National Council of the United National Independence Party, 19 April 1968.

20   For this argument, see Carolyn L. Baylies, *The State and Class Formation in Zambia* (University of Wisconsin, Ph.D., 1978).

21   See Paul Semonin, 'Nationalisations and Management in Zambia', *Maji Maji*, No. 1 (1971).

22   This discussion is based on C. Baylies, op. cit.; Morris Szeftel, *Conflict, Spoils and Class Formation in Zambia* (University of Manchester, Ph.D., 1978); and Karen Eriksen, 'Zambia: Class Formation and Detente', *Review of African Political Economy*, No. 9 (1978), pp. 18–26.

23   K. D. Kaunda, op. cit., p. 37.

24   United National Independence Party, *National Policies for the Next Decade 1974–1984* (Lusaka, 1973), p. 39.

25   ibid., p. 26; *First National Development Plan 1966–1970* (Lusaka, 1966), pp. 6–8, 33–6; and *Second National Development Plan 1972–1976* (Lusaka, 1971), pp. 19–20, 93–4.

26   Ann Seidman, 'The Distorted Growth of Import-Substitution Industry: The Zambian Case', *Journal of Modern African Studies*, 12, 4 (1974), pp. 601–31; and M. R. Bhagavan, *Zambia: Impact of Industrial Strategy on Regional Imbalance and Social Inequality* (Uppsala, 1978), Chap. 5.

27   Giovanni Arrighi, 'International Corporations, Labour Aristocracies, and Economic Development in Tropical Africa', in Robert I. Rhodes (ed.), *Imperialism and Underdevelopment: a Reader* (New York, 1970), p. 252.

28   *Third National Development Plan 1979–1983* (Lusaka, 1979), p. *v*.

29   *Report of the Committee on Parastatal Bodies* (Lusaka, 1979), p. 55.

30   Robin Fincham, 'Economic Dependence and the Development of Zambia', *Journal of Modern African Studies*, 18, 2 (1980), pp. 299–303.

31   See Morris Szeftel, 'Political Graft and the Spoils System in Zambia – the State as a Resource in Itself', *Review of African Political Economy*, No. 24 (1982), pp. 4–21.

32   For 'The Arusha Declaration and Self-Reliance', see Nyerere, op. cit., pp. 231–50.

33   See Michaela von Freyhold, 'The Post-Colonial State and Its Tanzanian Version', *Review of African Political Economy*, No. 8 (1977), pp. 86–9, which also presents an alternative view to the one given here regarding the promulgation of the Arusha Declaration.

34   For Nyerere's case for socialism in Tanzania, see 'The Rational Choice', in Julius K. Nyerere, *Freedom and Development. A Selection from Writings and Speeches 1968–1973* (Dar es Salaam, 1973), pp. 379–90.

35   See Cranford Pratt, *The Critical Phase in Tanzania 1945–1968. Nyerere and the Emergence of a Socialist Strategy* (Cambridge, 1976), for a detailed discussion.

36   John Loxley and John S. Saul, 'Multinationals, Workers and the Parastatals in Tanzania', *Review of African Political Economy*, No. 2 (1975), pp. 54–88.

37   Zaki Ergas, 'The State and Economic Deterioration: The Tanzanian Case', *Journal of Commonwealth and Comparative Politics*, 20, 3 (1982), pp. 286–308.

38   John S. Saul, 'African Socialism in One Country: Tanzania', in Giovanni Arrighi and John S. Saul, *Essays on the Political Economy of Africa* (New York, 1973), pp. 289, 290.

39   Loxley and Saul, op. cit., p. 61.

40   For this policy paper, see Nyerere, *Freedom and Socialism*, op. cit. pp. 337–66.

41   ibid., p. 348, emphasis in original.

42   For a description of how this move was made, see J. V. Mwapachu, 'Operation Planned Villages in Rural Tanzania', *The African Review*, 6, 1 (1976), pp. 1–16. See also Andrew Coulson, 'Agricultural Policies in Mainland Tanzania', *Review of African Political Economy*, No. 10 (1977), pp. 74–100; and Jannik Boesen, 'Tanzania: from Ujamaa to Villagisation', in Bismarck U. Mwansasu and Cranford Pratt (eds.), *Towards Socialism in Tanzania* (Dar es Salaam, 1979), pp. 125–44, for overall discussions.

43   See P. L. Raikes, 'Ujamaa and Rural Socialism', *Review of African Political Economy*, No. 3 (1975), pp. 33–52; and Michaela von Freyhold, *Ujamaa Villages in Tanzania. Analysis of a Social Experiment* (London, 1979).

44   For an alternative view to the one presented here, see Cranford Pratt, 'Democracy and Socialism in Tanzania', *Canadian Journal of African Studies*, 12, 3 (1978), pp. 424–5.

45   Issa G. Shivji, *Class Struggles in Tanzania* (Dar es Salaam, 1975), p. 75; and Susanne D. Mueller, 'Retarded Capitalism in Tanzania', in Ralph Miliband and John Saville, eds, *The Socialist Register 1980* (London, 1980), pp. 203–26.

46   S. S. Mushi, 'Popular Participation and Regional Development Planning: The Politics of Decentralized Administration', *Tanzania Notes and Records*, No. 83 (1978), pp. 63–97.

47   Freyhold, op. cit., Chap. 6.

48   See Yash Tandon, 'The Food Question in East Africa: A Partial Case Study of Tanzania', *Africa Quarterly*, 17, 4 (1978), pp. 5–45.

49   Ergas, op. cit., p. 299; and Mueller, op. cit., p. 218.

50   AIM Information Bulletin (Maputo), No. 42 (December, 1979). For a discussion of the experience in the liberated areas, see Barry Munslow, *Mozambique: The Revolution and its Origins* (London, 1983), Chap. 13.

51   This discussion is based on Peter Meyns, 'Liberation Ideology and National Development Strategy in Mozambique', *Review of African Political Economy*, No. 22 (1981), pp. 42–64.

52   John S. Saul, 'Frelimo and the Mozambique Revolution', in Arrighi and Saul, op. cit., p. 380.

53   See Peter Meyns, *Befreiung und Nationaler Wiederaufbau von Mozambique. Studien zu Politik und Wirtschaft 1960–1978* (Hamburg, 1979), pp. 81–4.

54   All quotations from Frelimo documents cited in Barry Munslow, 'The Liberation Struggle in Mozambique and the Origins of Post-Independence Political and Economic Policy', in Centre of African Studies, University of Edinburgh (ed.), *Mozambique* (Edinburgh, 1978).

55   Cited in Basil Davidson, 'The Revolution of People's Power: Notes on Mozambique, 1979', *Monthly Review*, 32, 3 (1980), pp. 77–8.

56   David and Marina Ottaway, *Afrocommunism* (New York, 1981), pp. 80–1.

57   Cited in *ibid.*, p. 87.

58   Cited in Munslow article, op. cit., p. 94.

59   This concluding discussion is based on S. F. Latham, 'About-turn in Mozambique', *The World Today*, 37, 2 (1981), pp. 69–73.

60   For a recent discussion on this subject from this perspective, see Dan Nabudere, *The Political Economy of Imperialism* (London, 1978).

61   Freyhold, 'The Post-Colonial State', op. cit., p. 85.

62   Steven Langdon, 'Multinational Corporations and the State in Africa', in José J. Villamil (ed.), *Transnational Capitalism and National Development: New Perspectives on Dependence* (Hassocks, 1979), p. 230.

Classes
and Politics

Africa is part of the capitalist world system and the capitalist mode of production has, during the course of the present century, become dominant in the continent. Social classes are basically determined by the mode of production and thus the configuration of classes found in Africa consists essentially of those classes that comprise the capitalist mode of production, namely, the bourgeoisie, the proletariat and the peasantry. As employed in this work, the concept of class denotes a grouping of individuals who share a common position in the process of production especially in regard to the ownership of the means of production. It is important to note that the class categories we adopt do not reflect the existence of homogeneous groups; classes are characterized by intra-class distinctions and segmentation and are comprised of various sections and 'fractions'. In addition, the concept of class does not necessarily imply that a particular class grouping possesses a distinctive class consciousness; a collective consciousness is a rare phenomenon and has seldom occurred in contemporary Africa.[1]

The mode of production in African countries underwent fundamental change during the colonial period with consequent implications for class formation. Capitalist production entailed a modification, and even replacement, of pre-capitalist relations and the emergence of a new class structure. At the time of independence, African countries possessed broadly similar class structures. The largest single class was that of the peasantry and there was also a small working class. Then there was the petty bourgeoisie, composed of those in petty-capitalist agriculture and small-scale trade. In addition there were those individuals in bureaucratic positions (teachers, clerks, civil servants) who constituted not a class but, more precisely, a status group. Conflicts between these groupings were minor during the colonial period. The main division was a racial one, that between Africans and Europeans. Since independence, however, class divisions have become politically significant and conflicts amongst the various African strata have attained considerable political importance.

We have argued in a previous chapter that politicians have been concerned with personal enrichment and individual accumulation. The mass of the people in the urban and rural areas hold similar views.

Attitudinal surveys have revealed that most villagers perceive politicians as untrustworthy, self-interested and dishonest.[2] The urban labouring poor also see the politico-economic system as unjust and view politicians and senior civil servants as predatory and oppressive. The unequal distribution of power and wealth resulting in a huge gap between senior state personnel and the masses has stimulated workers and peasants to demand reforms or even, at times, fundamental changes within the status quo. Moreover, workers and peasants have responded to their exploitation as producers by the state and capital, local as well as foreign. The class basis of such political actions by the poor and exploited classes is examined in this chapter. But there are also conflicts amongst the petty bourgeoisie, indigenous bourgeoisie, and state personnel as well as contradictions between these groupings and foreign capital and international aid agencies. These class divisions and their political expressions are also the subject of the present chapter.

Co-existent with class formation and evolving class consciousness during the colonial period was ethnic consciousness and identity. Ethnic consciousness was widely extant in both the rural and urban areas of colonial Africa and had, indeed, developed and evolved as a result of actions of colonial states (such as introducing administrative and political units which corresponded with ethnic groups; conflicts arose because of the unbalanced nature of development, or the unequal distribution of schools and infrastructures). But ethnic differences during the colonial period appear mainly to have become important politically when rival leaders, engaged in political competition, manipulated ethnicity for their own purposes. In situations, for instance, where the nationalist leaders were divided into rival political parties, they appealed to ethnic sentiments to win support for themselves. There was a class dimension to ethnic conflict and division which has continued in independent Africa. This dimension has already been considered in Chapter 2 and is examined further below.

The labouring poor in urban Africa

Historically, the organized working class played a key role in the political struggles of the advanced capitalist countries in western Europe in promoting the extension of democratic rights and the 'welfare state'. To what extent have workers in Africa played, or been able to play, a similar role in a movement for social justice?

The urban wage-earning force in Africa is still relatively small. Although the opportunities for wage employment have been increasing since independence, albeit slowly, the wage force as a whole has remained a minority of the total population. It is also generally a minority of the urban population, especially of the urban labour force. While small in size, urban wage-earners have achieved remarkable stability, particularly since the 1950s. This stable wage-labour force, however, remains only partially proletarianized. Most urban workers may intend to live and work in urban centres for long periods, but a majority of them still retain extensive links with the rural areas, to which many will eventually return. Nevertheless, to the extent that a wage-labour force has become stabilized in the towns, workers have sought to protect and advance their interests through collective organization. The degree of stability may not imply full proletarianization, but it does imply a strong commitment to wage employment and a heightened awareness on the part of workers of the need to defend their interests as working men and women.

To cater for the interests of urban wage-earners, various organizations have emerged. Of these the trade union has been the main workers' organization. Worker-oriented political parties have occasionally been started (such as the Sudanese Communist Party) but they have not been tolerated and have been severely repressed. And with the suppression generally of opposition parties, trade unions have represented the sole institutional means for advancing the interests of wage-earners and expressing popular discontent.

Trade unions, however, have generally been led by middle-class 'outsiders' and working-class membership and participation in them has been usually at a low level. This is particularly the case with unions at the national level. National union leaders are often estranged from the workers because of their higher incomes, different life-styles and the bureaucratization of union affairs on a national level. Unions have also invariably been subject to state control: governments have in various ways sought to control unions to ensure that they do not pose a threat to the government as well as the interests it serves. Moreover, there are many instances of workers having little or no confidence in their unions, which have been seen as betraying their interests and as having 'sold them out' to management and the state. Konings has shown how the Industrial and Commercial Workers Union (ICU) – the largest union in Ghana – has identified with the ruling group's developmental ideology by constantly exhorting workers to increase production and to avoid strike action (as the workers' contribution to national development), and has also adhered strictly to the 'official' bargaining structures to bring about economic gains within the existing system rather than assuming an overt political role through strike threats and actions. A large number of workers have therefore distrusted the union. As one worker remarked: 'National union officers, managers and government are bed-fellows in the exploitation of labour.'[3]

Yet although unions have to some extent not developed as genuine workers' organizations, they have been of some significance for wage-earners in the promotion of their interests. At times the headquarters of unions may be subordinated to the governing party but the union branches have not been taken over and have retained their independence. At other times branch unions have seceded from government-controlled national union organization and have challenged state power. Moreover, local branch leaders are usually much closer to union members and much more likely to identify with this rank and file and their 'consumptionist' demands rather than with government/management and the national unions' 'productionist' demands. Strike actions and protests have thus been organized by local unions, some of which have seriously affected the position of the ruling regimes.

But where unions have been tightly controlled and strikes constitutionally banned, workers have devised their own means of advancing their interests. Covert forms of labour protest should not be ignored in this context.[4] Informal modes of protest have taken various forms – absenteeism, theft, sabotage, work avoidance, slow work-rates – and have constituted an important expression of labour agitation, especially in coercive political systems. The passivity displayed by workers at times of acute socio-economic hardship can be explained in part by the resort to such covert and individual forms of protest. Nevertheless, overt and collective action has remained a key mode of protest by labour. This has been expressed either through the unions or by *ad hoc* organizations set up by the workers themselves which have opposed the official unions.

Whether through unions or not, workers have become involved not only in occupational or workplace issues but also in political agitation. Three broad types of working-class action may be distinguished in contemporary Africa.[5] The first type is the reformist one. In this case workers have been primarily concerned with industrial and economic grievances – wages, social benefits, working conditions, union and worker rights, and management behaviour – and are involved in bargaining with employers and government for incremental and piecemeal reforms. The aim has been to attain improvements within the existing system. The demands voiced have not been radical: workers have not challenged the political and socio-economic system. They have also been sectional in orientation, being concerned with the betterment of those making the demands rather than wage-earners as a whole. It has been the immediate self-interest of particular groups of workers that has been the focus of action rather than workers in general. Workers have generally resorted to collective bargaining to extract their industrial and economic gains. But at times strikes (and other forms of action) have been employed, usually as a last weapon for promoting workers' interests. However, strikes have only occurred occasionally, partly because participants in illegal strikes, especially those in vital industries, have generally been severely punished (incarceration of labour leaders and large-scale dismissals), and partly because workers prefer to resort to other covert, forms of action to protest against their exploitation. For instance, local union leaders may resort to go-slow action to demonstrate the workers' 'power' to management and to strengthen their bargaining position. All such agitation, however, should not be viewed as apolitical as it can, at times, pose a threat to managerial and governmental authority, as was evidenced by the violent industrial troubles in the Ghanaian mining industry from 1968 to 1970 and in 1977.

The second type of working class action – designated radical-democratic – entails action on the part of workers from different sectors (as in general strikes) or between a particular group of workers and the sub-proletariat that directly offers a challenge to state power. Such action has represented a form of urban populism embodying a critique of and strong antagonism towards the existing political and social order on the part of the labouring poor. In 1961 (and again in 1971) the port and rail workers of Sekondi-Takoradi in Ghana posed as the spokesmen of the poor 'common people' in the urban areas. They staged a 17-day strike against the Nkrumah government and 'its increasingly corrupt, autocratic and elitist character'. The railway and harbour workers and the sub-proletariat resented elite wealth, and the corruption and authoritarian rule of the CPP politicians, and this popular discontent erupted in a major political challenge to the government. Jeffries writes about the 1961 strike that the workers conceived of themselves as acting on behalf of all the 'common people' and, in turn, 'the urban poor of Sekondi-Takoradi looked to the more highly articulate and organized workers to lead expression of a generalized sense of social injustice and exploitation'. The widening socio-economic gap between the politico-administrative elite and the urban masses 'united virtually the whole Sekondi-Takoradi community in support of the strike'.[6] The strike was therefore political in conception: it was consciously directed against the government rather than management and was concerned not just with occupational and economic matters but with the policies and characteristics of the regime in power. Similar political action has occurred elsewhere in Africa. In Tanzania in 1971 there was a series of strikes in Dar es Salaam as workers called for more democracy and independence within the national trade union organization and greater workers' participation. In both the Ghanaian and Tanzanian examples we see workers speaking and acting with the urban masses. Through collective action such as general strikes, workers have challenged the authority of government and in some cases (as in the 1960s in the former French colonies of Dahomey, Congo [Brazzaville] and Upper Volta) brought about the collapse of unpopular regimes. But such action has not been concerned with workers assuming power themselves. Such radical–democratic action has not been guided by any kind of socialist-oriented philosophy or been imbued with an image of social revolution. It has been informed by social–democratic values and contrasts with the third type of working-class action – socialist–revolutionary – which has not arisen in Africa.

Much of the industrial action in contemporary Africa has been concerned with the reformist type of activity. It is consequently argued that workers possess only a limited consciousness of their position in society and that this is primarily concerned with short-run economic benefits. They may be conscious of themselves as workers (rather than as persons drawn from different ethnic groups) but this is often narrowed in practice to a group and not a class consciousness in that workers generally seek reforms for a particular section of workers rather than workers as a whole. And, moreover, they generally seek the improvement of the economic conditions of workers – known as economism – and their consciousness hardly extends beyond this search for short-range economic gains. Their ideology has been that of a group seeking to further its own specific interests against those of their employer within the industrial setting. Workers do not appear to be committed to a radical stance regarding the present system: their aims are to achieve reforms or incremental changes within the status quo. Nor have workers displayed much concern with the political character of the regime in power, whether it is capitalist or socialist. What they have evinced in particular is the desire that politicians be honest, prepared to acknowledge the workers and be concerned with improving their lot.

But it is not the case that African urban workers have been capable only of this lower-level consciousness. In some parts of Africa, segments of workers have evolved a second level of consciousness – often termed a populist or radical–democratic (non-revolutionary) political orientation – which has transcended economism and reformism. This second level has entailed the identification of a group to which the interest of one's own group is opposed. Such identification has typically been in terms of 'the big men' (the rich and powerful) rather than in terms of a specific class. And the rich and powerful 'they' are those who advance themselves by cheating 'us', the poor people. In Ghana during a period of intense union-government conflict in 1971 commercial workers wore badges conveying a sentiment widely shared by the urban working poor: 'Monkey De Work, Baboon De Chop' (small men do the work, big men eat). Moreover, this sort of consciousness is not an exclusively working-class one: it is populist because it often brings together workers and the sub-proletariat and emphasizes the virtues of the common man fighting against a succession of big men. But it is also not revolutionary. Workers do not possess a clear vision of an alternative socio-economic and political system, instead, they advocate the establishment of a government that is concerned with their lot and is not elitist, corrupt and repressive. Such a consciousness entails chiefly protest and rebellion against corrupt individuals and groups rather than collective political action to take over and restructure society.

Finally there is the revolutionary working-class consciousness entailing the identification of an economically dominant class enemy and the vision of an alternative society which can only be brought about through the overthrow of existing institutions. But this is a rare type of consciousness and a revolutionary proletariat has not emerged in sub-Saharan Africa.

At present, it can be concluded that the working class evinces at most a radical–democratic consciousness while the predominant orientation has been that of economism whereby workers have tended to forgo any overt political role in favour of concentration upon the advance and defence of their narrow economic and workplace interests.

One argument put forward to explain the moderate political role of workers has been that the better-off, more skilled section of the wage-earning force has, because of its privileged position, been co-opted by the ruling sectors into the existing order. This is the 'labour-aristocracy' thesis.[7] It is held that the skilled (and semi-skilled) segment of the working class constitutes a more privileged group vis-à-vis the urban poor – unskilled workers and the sub-proletariat. The interests of the higher-paid workers are closer to those of the ruling group than to those of the urban poor and they also seek to defend the privileged economic and social position they have attained. But this thesis has been challenged on empirical grounds (as well as theoretical ones – it is vague and imprecise).[8] The income differentials are not as large as has been claimed and although differences exist they are negated by the larger size of the urban household of better-off workers and the remittances from urban to rural households. Moreover, the more highly paid workers are usually not separated from the poorer urban groups either residentially or socially.[9] In addition, the differences that do exist within the lower-income group in the urban areas pale into insignificance and appear extremely trivial compared with the vast and mounting economic and social distance between the mass of low-paid workers and the elite of politicians and senior civil servants. Furthermore, the skilled manual workers have been, thus far, the most radical force in African politics and have played a leading role among the urban poor in the struggle against an inegalitarian order. In his study of workers in western Nigeria, Peace has examined the factors that have made workers identify 'downwards' with the urban poor (and demonstrated the existence of a 'populist' consciousness among workers) as well as depicted the strong degree of support by the urban poor of protests by skilled workers.[10]

Other arguments regarding the moderate political role of urban workers, although also susceptible to some criticism, provide, in combination, a more plausible explanation. One argument is that there are various factors that foster tensions and conflicts between workers and other sections of the urban poor. For example, the workers mistrust the presence of an 'industrial reserve army' that threatens their own security of employment, exercises a downward pressure on wages, and creates competition for work throughout the whole workforce. The consequence of the existence of large numbers of unemployed is to curb the militancy of the lower-paid workers in the private sector. A second argument revolves around workers being constantly exposed to the value system and ideology of the dominant classes in society. The value system in most, if not all, African countries supports individual competition and success, social mobility, respect and admiration for those who have attained wealth; while official ideologies such as *ujamaa* socialism in Tanzania, or humanism in Zambia, or Kenyan socialism, or Nigerian national revolution have either not questioned or have not attacked the emergent class structure. A third argument, related to the second one, is that workers often aspire to become self-employed entrepreneurs in the petty commodity sector. Indeed, a small number of workers are already active in this sector. Such petty bourgeois aspirations retard the development of a radical working-class consciousness. A fourth argument attributes the accommodationist role of workers' organizations to the general absence of a radical/revolutionary ideology and leadership. The transition to a revolutionary consciousness does not come about of itself, spontaneously. It is produced among the working class by revolutionaries. But in Africa there are hardly any radical parties and revolutionaries have been quickly repressed. The only organizations that exist to guide and influence the workers pursue ideologies that are reformist and within the present status quo, and the unions have also been reluctant to undertake politicization of the rank and file.

Finally, we may mention an argument in regard to the non-wage-earners, who account for the majority of the urban population in much of Africa. These are the self-employed in the 'informal' sector (artisans, small-scale traders and craftsmen, and workers in personal and domestic services) and the unemployed and 'lumpen' elements. Although some have viewed non-wage-earners as possibly spearheading urban revolution,[11] the reality of individualistic and competitive work situations of these elements of the urban poor has retarded the development of solidarity and militated against effective political organization. Not only have they been difficult to mobilize, but ethnic and religious affiliations have often reduced the potential for collective action. The consciousness of the urban poor has been rudimentary in the absence of external leadership and organization, notably from wage-earners.[12]

The peasantry

Although comprising much the largest social grouping and providing much of the wealth of the state, the peasantry as a social force in politics has been decidedly weak in contemporary Africa. In some parts of the world during the present century the peasants have become a revolutionary force; in China and Vietnam the great revolutions of the twentieth century were, to be an important extent, peasant wars or peasant revolutions. The participation of the peasantry in revolutionary struggles was also not absent in Africa; it was evident in the ex-Portuguese colonies, where wars of national liberation occurred,[13] and in Kenya during the Mau Mau struggle. Nevertheless, in sub-Saharan Africa there is much scepticism about the revolutionary potential of the peasantry in contemporary politics. Divided and demobilized the peasants have hardly constituted much of a political force of any sort in Africa and have hardly posed a threat to post-colonial regimes. The peasants have been Africa's silent majority.

Various reasons underlie such assertions.[14] Population pressure on the land has not been as acute in the rural areas of Africa as in other continents; the threat to peasant existence has not therefore been sufficient to evoke mass rural disaffection and agitation. Secondly, there exist social and cultural relationships – especially kinship and ethnic identities – which divide the peasants and prevent them from thinking (and organizing) in class terms; peasant politics has often been localized and expressed in regional or tribal terms. Peasant class-consciousness, or a sense of common identity, has also been inhibited by other factors. Prime among these is the heterogeneity of the peasantry; it is clear that it is not a single and homogeneous whole but is internally differentiated (composed of the rich, medium, poor, and landless peasants). The vertical patron–client networks extant throughout the rural countryside have also prevented the development of horizontal class loyalites and have brought the rural masses under the influence of central politicians through local 'big men'. The absence in much of Africa of an indigenous landed aristocracy has further prevented peasants from evolving a common focus of loyalty. And, moreover, the sheer problem of communication between isolated and dispersed settlements and the large number of illiterate peasants has impeded their ability to combine in a coherent political formation.

Thirdly, the widespread absence of the acute degree of tyranny and misery that provoke a peasant revolt has been linked with the absence of cadres to crystallize and focus whatever peasant discontent has existed. Even if one accepts that conditions for the peasantry have not been too oppressive, at least it would appear that peasants have generally lacked effective leadership to mobilize and direct them politically. Being largely illiterate, peasants have not appeared capable of forming an organization of their own and leading it themselves. During the colonial period, a rural petty bourgeoisie (composed of richer peasants, small-scale traders and farmers) linked the mass of the poor and middle peasants to the urban-based nationalists. But this rural political leadership had also begun to break away from peasant status and was incorporating petty-bourgeois aspirations. It began to evince a petty-capitalist orientation and in the post-colonial period it has, through its ideological bent, become more closely attached to the petty bourgeoisie as a whole and increasingly remote from the peasants. The result of this has not been so much that peasants are no longer represented politically by persons from different class backgrounds (elite rural politicians) but that the rural organizers have, through their leadership, often been able to deflect peasant agitation from peasant political purposes to serve their own interests.[15] Leadership of peasant agitation has often come from outside and the peasants have been unable to assume their own leadership.

Finally, it is important to note that governments have employed techniques to further the process of rural political demobilization. Rural producers often have grievances – especially those relating to low prices for their products or limited access to agricultural inputs – for which the state is held responsible. Through coercion and other means, governments have repressed those who have attempted to organize the rural producers in opposition to the policies of the government; they have thus prevented the mobilization of the peasants. Governments have also sought to separate the interests of potential rural leaders – the larger farmers, traders – from those of the mass of the rural populace. Through privileged access to subsidized farm inputs and in other ways, governments have induced larger farmers to see their interests as lying apart from those of the majority of the rural population and more akin to those of the regime in power. Furthermore, governments have engineered a pattern of politics in the African countryside whereby the 'politics of the pork barrel supplant the politics of class action'. Rural dwellers are led to focus on securing particular benefits from the state authorities – jobs, loans, mechanical equipment, permits – rather than pursuing their collective interests. Repression, co-option, and the promotion of competition and conflict for particular improvements: such have been the techniques at the heart of the process of rural demobilization.[16]

The marked political passivity of the mass of peasants, especially the poorer, small-scale agriculturalists, has been widely remarked upon. Small peasants have presented hardly any serious opposition to post-colonial governments in Africa. Yet peasants have not always been politically inert. At times they have resisted the exactions of the state, particularly when such exactions have been sufficiently onerous as to threaten to deprive them of the resources required to maintain their way of life. Schatzberg has vividly described the acute sufferings of peasants in rural Zaire – consequent upon low producer prices, inability of government to buy crops, excessive taxation, financial pressures of officialdom, bad facilities and so on – and portrayed the local administrative system as 'a driving force behind a vast system of rural exploitation, oppression, and violence'.[17] Such conditions have spawned peasant resistance.

In discussing peasant reactions, covert forms of peasant resistance to exploitation by the state should not be neglected. When economic impositions have become intolerable, peasants have reacted in various informal ways. Some have 'voted with their feet'. In Zaire, for instance, many villagers have fled to the deep forests or the river islands to avoid the burdens, agricultural and financial, of local officialdom. Others have smuggled their produce across national borders to evade lower government-controlled prices; while many have responded to low prices by simply abandoning the cultivation of specific commercial crops and reverting to subsistence farming. Such modes of protest have been common, for example, among the peanut-producing peasants in Senegal in their reactions to the onerous impositions of the state marketing structure. In this regard it is worth noting as well that the Senegalese peanut producers 'have had their own remarkably effective and rurally based organization. More than half (very possibly two-thirds) of peanut producers are affiliated to the Mouride brotherhood, a Sufi Moslem structure . . . [which has] emerged as the principal vehicle for the organized expression of peasant bitterness.' During the early years of the recent Sahelian drought (in the early 1970s), peasants, on the advice of the brotherhood, withdrew from peanut cultivation in favour of millet. This resulted in a threat to the government's tax base – heavily reliant on peanuts – which was sufficiently serious to prompt the authorities to almost double the producer price. O'Brien states that for the 'peanut peasants after 1973, the Mouride brotherhood has proved the efficacy of a bizarre and theatrical form of trade unionism. Mouride saints have constituted a body of rural leadership.'[18] Yet the Mouride saints have essentially acted as rural patrons organizing and mobilizing the rural masses to serve their own interests; the rural masses themselves have been largely passive politically. But apart from covert forms of resistance – guided or not by rural patrons – peasants have demonstrated on occasion some capacity for collective organization and collective action. Politically oriented collective action of a direct nature has occurred from time to time and has given some political potency to the demands of the non-literate, non-capitalist peasants. In movements of peasant resistance, arising out of specific and pressing rural grievances, the voice of the lower reaches of the peasantry has been articulated. And peasants have been able to organize themselves and express their collective interests under their own leadership.

Such collective action has often assumed a violent guise. More formal and constitutional avenues have not been unavailable. They have, however, been dominated in the main by the educated minority of farmers and rural capitalists, who have controlled such institutions as co-operatives, farmers' unions, and local government authorities, primarily to promote their private ends rather than to forward mass goals. Very rarely have such institutions gained large-scale support. This contrasts with those movements which have mobilized mass support and have been closely committed to mass peasant objectives. Direct action by peasants, where it has occurred, has often ensued from the failure of formal institutions to voice peasant interests. And in organizing themselves peasants have revealed the consciousness and ability to resist exploitation and oppression.

Peasant unrest has erupted in open violence in spontaneous or more organized form. Peasants often resort to violent and informal demonstrations. General unrest in the eastern region of Chad exploded into a spontaneous *jacquerie* in the 1965 tax riots in Mangalmé that led to over five hundred deaths. Decalo writes that the riots 'were directly precipitated by crass maladministration, and especially by the illegal trebling of local taxes by corrupt officials who pocketed the difference. The revolt was further fanned by . . . [a] decision to increase the head tax, extended to women as well, and coupled with a compulsory "development" contribution.'[19] As with other such spontaneous outbursts, however, the initial explosion was short-lived. Spontaneous resistance appears to have had little effect on ending corrupt government and the plight of the peasants has hardly been alleviated.

Organized resistance – peasant rebellions – have been an even rarer phenomenon in contemporary African politics. Two such revolts are worthy of mention. In 1964 a large and organized rebellion began in the Kwilu Province of Zaire. Fox *et al.* describe the rebellion as 'a revolutionary attempt to correct some of the abuses and injustices by which large segments of the population of the region felt oppressed'. As with many other peasant rebellions in Africa this century, it exhibited characteristics of a religious and political millenial movement. It was, in fact, similar to the various messianic religious movements that had grown up in 'colonial-type situations at the moment when the people subjugated by the regime begin to be conscious enough about their shared plight and indignant enough about it to wish to collectively liberate themselves from it'.[20] The so-called Agbekoya rebellion which erupted in western Nigeria in late 1968 also exemplifies organized and collective peasant resistance. The smallholding peasants 'saw themselves exploited and oppressed by a Government which refused to pay fair prices for their cocoa, sent corrupt officials to persecute them, denied them the benefits and amenities which they had been promised, and now demanded higher taxes when the farmers simply could not earn enough to pay them'.[21] The Agbekoya ('resistance against oppression') was a populist movement of the poorer, non-literate peasants which sought primarily to correct abuses by employing direct action under its own leadership.[22]

Like other populist movements, the Kwilu and Agbekoya rebellions had as their prime objectives the correction of abuses which had led to an acute degree of tyranny and misery. These rebellions were partly successful in redressing specific and pressing grievances; some concessions were secured from the government through acts of violence. Like other mass peasant organizations, Agbekoya and Kwilu did not go beyond such reformist aims to end peasant dependence on external markets and subordination to the state. All they sought to achieve (often with some success) were limitations on their own exploitation. Peasants have not been concerned with the revolutionary transformation of their society or the seizure of state power. Although clearly depicting class consciousness, such agrarian populism was not imbued with class war and with the destruction of the social order. In such movements the peasants have shown their continuing dependence on the government for the improvement of their lot and the alleviation of their sufferings. They have thus revealed their inability and lack of means (education, leadership, resources) to change their society of their own accord.[23]

Populist politics and ethnic movements

If workers and peasants have rarely been able to organize politically in coherent class movements, so too have they been unable to unite in a common political movement. In spite of continuing close ties between the urban masses and the rural peasants, these have not led to the emergence of a wider populist consciousness and political action. Also limited has been the exploitation of a generalized sense of discontent across society as a whole by politicians seeking mass support. During the colonial period the mobilization of the masses by tapping a miscellany of grievances among the rural and urban popular strata was widely extant in the 1950s. Since independence, however, politicians have generally tended to make their appeals for popular support along other and narrower lines, especially ethnic ones. Appeals along populist lines are more likely in multi-party systems and the widespread abolition of competitive party politics has doubtless been an important reason for their widespread absence in independent Africa. They do exist, however, in the few countries having multi-party politics. One example may be cited from Zambia, prior to the establishment of a one-party state there in 1973. Factional conflict within the ruling party UNIP resulted in the formation of the UPP in 1971. The UPP emerged at a time when Zambia was in the throes of an economic crisis. There was considerable public economic discontent consequent upon a rising cost of living, rural decline, and mounting urban unemployment. At the same time there was a growing awareness of the wide differences in income and material standards of living between the masses and the elite. Popular discontent provided the potential for an appeal along populist lines, and to some extent the UPP played upon popular dissatisfaction. 'Independence is good,' declared the UPP leader, 'but it is meaningless and useless if it does not bring fruits to the masses.' But the appeal was a limited one: it was directed primarily to an urban mass constituency and was also accompanied by appeals along ethnic or regional lines to obtain further popular support.

To be sure skilled workers have, as we have seen, spoken for a constituency larger than that of the unionized workers alone. In Ghana the TUC in the period 1969–72 laid claim to representing the mass of the people. In the absence of an official opposition that was representative of the 'common people', the unions saw themselves as the 'watchdogs' or the 'eyes and ears' of society. But this identification was between workers and the urban poor: the unions sought to speak for an urban mass constituency and there were few political links with the rural peasants. A wider populist consciousness (the common people as against the 'big men') has hardly emerged or been reflected in populist political action.

In Chapter 2 the argument was made that ethnicity is a divisive tool manipulated by politicians in furtherance of their own interests. A contrary argument, strongly propounded, has been that there have been situations in which the main motivation of political action has been ethnic; where both leaders and followers, belonging to the same ethnic group, have been united in a movement seeking the promotion of ethnic interests.[24] Such movements have transcended class differences and acquired considerable popular support by bringing together workers and peasants. Their importance politically is not to be gainsaid and, in a few states – Angola (1975–84), Burundi (1966–72), Chad (1966–84), and Nigeria (1967–70) – ethnic considerations have resulted in large-scale civil upheavals.

Valid as such an interpretation may be, it does not take into account the fact that the mobilization of mass bases along ethnic lines involves a class dimension. This is not to deny that mass-based ethnic attachments have transcended class identifications. But as the following brief discussion seeks to show, there is an intricate interrelationship between ethnicity and class underlying political action rooted in ethnic divisions and ethnic conflict.

The politics of ethnic conflict during the first decade of Nigeria's independence have often been seen as stemming from the three-region federal structure the country inherited from British colonial rule. The three regions corresponded with three major ethnic groups – the Hausa-Fulani, the Yoruba, and the Igbo – and political parties evolved along ethnic and regional lines. Each region was controlled by a particular political party deriving its support from the majority ethnic group of the region. In the struggle for political power – at the regional and federal levels – ethnic divisions were politicized and Nigeria's first Republic was eventually destroyed as politics became fiercely polarized around ethnicity. Such a view helps us to understand the civil upheavals leading to civil war in Nigeria during the 1960s. But for a more complete understanding one has also to consider the class forces that shaped the pattern of ethnic and political conflict.

As elsewhere in sub-Saharan Africa, Nigerians have seen political office as an open ticket to wealth and status. Once power had been attained the dominant party in each region used regional powers to enhance the material wealth of its members and supporters. The dominant regional parties also sought to acquire political control over the federation and its financial resources. The party that controlled the federal state, the NPC, used its political power to advance the position of politicians and state personnel from the north and to enhance their interests in competition with those from the east and west regions. Because control of the state – at the regional and federal level – was the basis of social mobility, those in power also sought to retain power. Each of the three dominant regional parties employed various means – patronage, repression, electoral fraud – to entrench their rule. At the federal level, the prime strategy for political success was an appeal to ethnic attachments and sentiments. Strong ethnic attachments existed among the rural and urban masses and there was also socio-economic competition between ethnic groups. These perceptions of difference and conflicting interests were heightened by politicians. It was the politicians who initiated ethnic recriminations and appealed for support along ethnic lines, largely for their own ends. The major ethnic conflicts during Nigeria's first Republic were thus rooted in elite conflict. They were the product of manipulation by politicians locked in bitter struggle for control of state power and resources.[25]

The above argument notwithstanding, ethnicity has some independence as a political factor and ethnic conflict has emerged apart from the motives of politicians. Ethnic differences and divisions can be important politically in their own right and cannot always be subsumed under the phenomenon of class and elite conflict. This type of ethnicity, however, is not given much consideration in this work. Such ethnic patterns of conflict and division are not entirely unimportant – as can be seen in the serious civil disorders in various African countries – but they are not generally of much importance in explaining many areas of political activity. Attention to social classes, on the other hand, can contribute much more to our understanding of political action in contemporary Africa.

The propertied classes and state personnel

The growth of the number of Africans among the petty bourgeoisie as well as the emergence of an indigenous bourgeoisie have been important aspects of class formation in post-colonial Africa.

The category of petty bourgeoisie includes all those owners of small capital who are also the sole operators of that capital. It consequently includes small-scale farmers, petty traders, artisans and shopkeepers. These are, in other words, small property owners. The category of bourgeoisie, on the other hand, encompasses those owners of large capital (and includes therefore indigenous and foreign capitalists) who are not directly involved in the labour process. During the colonial period indigenous owners of substantial capital were few and confined to relatively small enterprises in agriculture and commerce. The most dominant members of an owning class were foreign. But since independence the ranks of indigenous capitalists have swelled considerably and some have acquired ownership of large-scale and multiple enterprises in various economic sectors. An important source of recruitment of the indigenous bourgeoisie has been the upper echelons of the party, civil service and parastatals. Few members of the petty bourgeoisie, it would appear, have become more substantial capitalists. It has usually been those in political or government office who have been able to enhance their own mobility. Access to the spoils of office have provided politicians and senior civil servants with the means to acquire property and business interests and move into the bourgeoisie. In many African countries, and especially those whose economic policies have laid emphasis on private capitalism and private enterprise, there has been a considerable overlap between bureaucratic and political position and private interests with state personnel simultaneously having business interests. Nevertheless, an indigenous bourgeoisie has remained a small component of the class of capitalists as a whole. African countries are still dominated by foreign capital and, occasionally, by settler capital.

A third category that may be distinguished is that of state and party functionaries. This group is not strictly a class, as functionaries do not occupy a position in the production process. Included in this category are political leaders, top level state officials and executives of parastatals. State personnel thus include two main components: first, high-level government officials (in the civil service, military and police) and senior parastatal managers; and, secondly, party members such as top party officials, leading politicians and members of legislatures. Senior state personnel often have much in common with members of the bourgeoisie. Senior bureaucrats and leading politicians often aspire to join the private sector as property owners. Indeed, as we have indicated, many have acquired business interests whilst holding public office. Similarly, property owners have emerged from the upper levels of the civil service and the party. It is important to note that members of the bourgeoisie (and petty bourgeoisie) have not only been drawn from the ranks of politicians and civil servants but have also emerged through the patronage of the state. The emergent owning group has relied on the state for the acquisition of management experience and capital for investment as well as for subsequent access to loan facilities, licences and contracts.[26]

These three categories therefore share various common interests as well as having a common background; but there are also strains in their relations. Contradictions often arise among the propertied classes (petty bourgeoisie, bourgeoisie) and state and party personnel. These contradictions have informed much of the politics of Africa since independence, and we are here concerned with the nature of these tensions and their political implications.

The sources of division have been various; and all would appear to have a strong economic basis. The propertied classes and state personnel have been united in having 'economic nationalism' as their goal – the need to secure as large a share of the economy in national hands – as well as on the general goal of national economic development. But as to how these objectives should be attained, through state-directed economic activity involving the creation of public enterprises or through the promotion of national capitalist development, this has been a matter of some contention. The propertied classes have naturally advocated the furtherance of private domestic ownership, whereas state personnel have, in a number of countries, inclined more towards state ownership. In practice the two approaches have not been mutually exclusive. In Zambia, for instance, both have been pursued simultaneously in the so-called 'mixed economy'. But the balance struck between the two has aroused much friction. Secondly, even where agreement has existed on the overall economic approach – as in countries pursuing primarily national capitalism – friction has occurred. In Kenya, for instance, competition has taken place between small and large capital. Thirdly, there are countries where the state personnel have become increasingly concerned with their own 'reproduction' as a class. In Tanzania and Mozambique, for example, the state machinery has grown enormously in size and the state has become preponderant in economic affairs. Control of the economy by means of control over numerous state enterprises has constituted a way of furthering the corporate interests of state personnel as a whole in relation to other classes. Where propertied classes (such as 'kulaks' and agrarian capitalists) continue to exist, conflicts have arisen between them and the state regarding their respective economic interests. Finally, there have been struggles among the state personnel themselves, revolving around appropriation and the spoils of office as well as ideological and other divisions.

A major source of friction – typically in those states laying emphasis on public enterprise – has been that between the petty bourgeoisie and the state. Baylies has examined the case of the Zambia National Council of Commerce and Industry (ZNCCI) as an example of such friction. Members of the ZNCCI were small commercial or service industry capitalists who appealed to the state for aid in their individual enterprises. They requested the government to provide credit (especially to oust settler capital) and grant them representation on decision-making councils. Failure on the part of the Zambian government to accede to the demands of the petty bourgeoisie resulted in much political agitation and political division. Moreover, there were tensions between members of small indigenous private capital and state capital. In Zambia there have been certain areas in which the state parastatal, Indeco (the Industrial Development Corporation) has been brought into potential competition with indigenous capital. Indeco's involvement in commerce has been a source of grievance to private traders. Indeco has set up a chain of shops throughout the rural areas which have competed with those of retail traders. Competition between a parastatal and small Zambian business-men has subsequently been transferred to the political sphere resulting in much bickering and protest.[27] According to two writers, one of the major class struggles in Tanzania today is also that between the bureaucracy (based in the civil service, parastatals and in appointive positions in the ruling party) and the capitalist-oriented traders and 'kulaks'. Opportuni-ties for private trade and wealth have been undermined by the expanding role of the state in economic activity. State controls have led to restrictions on the growth of a bourgeoisie and to a decline in the power of traders and 'kulaks', leading to antagonism between them and the party and state bureaucrats.[28] In Mali under the US regime in the 1960s the 'creation of a public economic sector . . . brought the bureaucrats into competition with private business, particularly with the native traders'. Meillassoux continues: 'A riot of merchants supported by some leaders of the former PSP took place in July 1963. The alleged leaders were sent to jail and sentenced to death . . .'[29] Similarly in Nigeria, state involvement in commerce and manufacturing threatened the intermediary position between foreign capital and the domestic market which local businessmen occupied. 'The full rhetoric of unfettered private enterprise was marshalled by the Chamber of Commerce against state capitalist usurpation of their middlemen's activities.'[30]

A second source of friction that has occurred in a number of states, especially those with a large public enterprise sector, has been that between large-scale indigenous capital and the state. Private capital in Zambia has, since the 1970s, been continually urging the government to bring to an end state takeovers of companies, and to transfer companies to private hands; to give greater encouragement to local private enterprise; to invite foreign private involvement; and to direct state economic policy primarily towards a more capitalist orientation. On the other hand the ruling party UNIP has articulated, and to an extent implemented, a populist programme. Although it has experienced serious decline as a mass organization, 'UNIP still seeks to legitimate itself as a mass party and as one that furthers the interests of the weak and the poor.' As a consequence, writes Szeftel,

> a proportion of the surplus continued to be diverted directly or indirectly towards these groups through state subsidies on staple commodities and essential inputs (such as fertilizer for agriculture). And a wide variety of welfare measures, including free health facilities and education have continued to be provided. The Party rhetoric has continued to include denunciations of

capitalism [and advocation of socialism] . . . Inevitably, conflicts arise between Government and businessmen.[31]

Similarly, in Nigeria, Osoba argues that some of 'the most antagonistic contradictions exist between the bureaucratic bourgeoisie (whether military or civilian) and the business bourgeoisie'. This, he contends, is because the former 'have some awareness of a constituency of accountability' whereas the latter 'do not feel the pressure of such a constituency'. A 'classic case of such a contradiction' has arisen whenever the government, in recognition of the dependence of the economy on foreign capital, has called upon Nigerians to assume the ownership and control of the economy rather than merely operating as agents for foreign economic interests. Yet Nigerian businessmen have continued to voice the need for foreign investment and have urged countries such as Britain to take, according to a speech delivered by the president of the Nigerian Chamber of Commerce, 'a more aggressive and dynamic interest in Nigeria. Britain should be pressing hard to regain the trading and economic leadership which she seems so tamely to have abandoned.' Osoba concludes that this 'kind of blatant contradiction of stated government policy position on the national economy' indicates that the government would find implementation of policy 'extremely hard, if not impossible, as a great deal of its success would depend on the willing and active co-operation of the Nigerian business bourgeoisie'.[32]

Strains between the dominant and smaller 'fractions' of the indigenous owning class constitute a third main contradiction, one that has been particularly prevalent in those states favouring private enterprise economies. In regard to Kenya, for example, Swainson writes of 'considerable struggle between the larger businessmen and small-scale traders to obtain the most significant distributorships for goods'.[33] Those engaged in small trading have also collided with the larger-scale capitalists in negotiating loan capital from Kenya's state banks. Indeed, the conflict has occurred over a wide range of issues:

over access to land [i.e. on the question of ceilings on land holdings] . . . over the proportion of state finance capital – credit – to be distributed beyond the ranks of the bourgeoisie; over the degree of protection to be given to retail trade at the expense of wholesale trade and manufacturing; over the bias of fiscal policy towards either large scale, technically advanced capital, or small scale, technically backward ('labour intensive') capital, etc.[34]

Leys writes that in 'many respects the indigenous bourgeoisie's struggle with the petty bourgeoisie was more intense and critical than its struggle with the workers . . .' It was the KPU which voiced the interests of the 'small man' as against 'the rich' up to the time of its banning in 1969; and since then various backbenchers belonging to the ruling KANU party (such as J. M. Kariuki, who was assassinated under mysterious circumstances in 1975) have ventilated a populist ideology including the interests of small property. The politics of such division has been reflected in the outlawing of opposition parties, assassination of 'populist' leaders and the neutralization by other means of the political spokesmen of the petty bourgeoisie.

A fourth set of antagonisms are those that have emerged within the category of state personnel. Struggles among state personnel have already been identified in Chapter 2: these were political conflicts or internal fights between the 'ins' and 'outs', that is, over who should control the state apparatus in order to enjoy the fruits of power. But it is also important to note that conflicts along other lines – particularly ideological – have resulted in serious political divisions. In Tanzania, for instance, it is often argued that a distinction needs to be made between the bureaucrats and parastatal managers on the one hand and the politicians and party leaders on the other. Saul writes that there has been a struggle between those 'who seek to consolidate the neo-colonial set up and those who are moved, increasingly, to challenge it'. It has been, he argues, the political functionaries that have generally enunciated the more progressive measures such as the Arusha Declaration package of policies and Mwongozo (the TANU Guidelines of 1971).[35]

A final contradiction to be noted is that between the indigenous bourgeoisie and state personnel on the one hand and the international bourgeoisie on the other. The initial concerns of African businessmen after independence revolved around the exclusion of settler or immigrant capital from certain economic, particularly trading, activities. These concerns – involving conflicts with Asians, Europeans and Lebanese – typically aroused much agitation and were usually resolved in favour of indigenous businessmen. Over time, conflicts arose regarding the relative share of profits taken by foreign and indigenous capitalists in the 'neo-colonial' economies, chief among them Kenya, Nigeria and the Ivory Coast. The emergent national bourgeoisie as well as state capital, although weak economically in relation to the international bourgeoisie, have been able to wrest important concessions from international capital. Domestic African capital (private and state) has not been a mere tool of international capital. In its struggle against the dominance of international capital, African capital has, as indicated in Chapter 3, used its political hegemony over the state apparatus to extend its interests.

Tensions therefore occur among the state personnel and propertied elements and may at times erupt into serious conflict. There certainly is no unanimity of views among them and, as the above examples have shown, there are and can be serious differences between them on a range of issues. Political turmoil in Africa has ensued largely from such 'intra-elite' conflicts and divisions rather than from elite–mass cleavages in society. Indeed, internecine conflicts have been the source of much of the political instability in contemporary Africa.

Yet the differences that exist are rarely deep and fundamental and there is little sense of permanent hostility between the various sections. The differences, moreover, are overshadowed, to some extent, by a basic community of interests. Common attitudes transcend, to varying degrees, their specific divisions. In fact, this entire category of people has developed a sense of mutual solidarity. 'They are, in short, conscious of their elevated position in the social order, intent on defending it, and more than willing to accord each other the *avantages* and other courtesies that seem to go with their rank.' Solidarity has ensued from a collective interest in maintaining the status quo. In regard to Zaire, Schatzberg also argues that this higher strata of society has an 'adversary' relationship vis-à-vis the less privileged sections of the population. It exhibits a certain scorn for its less fortunate fellow citizens and also fears that it could be a target for the wrath of the masses.[36] Solidarity among the disparate dominant elements has ensued from a collective need to secure the present order against challenge from below.

What Miliband has argued about the states in the advanced capitalist world would appear to be applicable to the large majority of African states: 'the politics of advanced capitalism have been about different conceptions of how to run the *same* economic and social system, and not about radically different social systems'.[37] Rarely have the dominant elements in Africa been concerned with achieving a wholesale transformation of society into an entirely different social order. The politics of the dominant elements has been concerned with the pursuit of reforms within the ambit of the existing system rather than seeking to supersede that system. To be sure such politics can be the source of much political strife. But a basic harmony of interest exists conducive to fostering a degree of 'intra-elite' cohesion.

Many have insisted that the primary conflict in advanced capitalist countries is that between capitalists and wage-earners. Whether this is the case or not, it would appear that in contemporary Africa there are other forms of class conflict which are important politically and should not be neglected. But one thing appears to be constant. Antagonisms occur between (as well as within) classes but do not necessarily turn the different classes into mutually hostile ones. In Africa, as well, rarely have conflicts between social aggregates of different kinds been concerned with achieving the wholesale transformation of society into an entirely new social order. All of the classes have sought specific reforms within the prevailing system rather than achieve the overthrow of that system. Do the military revolutionaries constitute an exception?

The military revolutionaries

Military coups have occurred in Africa as a result of struggles for the control of state power. But such struggles have taken place within the ruling group of civilian politicians and military officers. Coups have represented palace revolutions. Recent years, however, have witnessed a different sort of military takeover. Countries such as Ethiopia and Ghana have seen the emergence to power of the lower ranks and junior officers, whose overthrow of the incumbents of state power has entailed a revolutionary transformation of the social order. These have constituted the military revolutionaries.

The military revolts of the lower ranks in a few African countries, such as Zanzibar in 1964 and Ethiopia in 1974 (and perhaps Liberia in 1980), were designed to secure the overthrow of feudal systems. Revolutionary changes followed the ousting of the ruling aristocracies. But it is the coups which have occurred in Ghana in recent years which are our main concern here as they mark a development which could assume wider application elsewhere in Africa. The abortive coup in Kenya in 1982 as well as the successful coup in Upper Volta in 1983 reflected in many ways the features of the coups which took place in Ghana in 1979 and 1981.

Since independence in 1957, Ghana has experienced a number of coups. The ones which occurred in the years 1966, 1972 and 1978 were typical of military takeovers in other parts of Africa in that they arose out of conflicts within the ruling groups and were the consequence of actions of senior officers. The coup of 4 June 1979, however, was the work of the junior officers and lower ranks. Led by Flight-Lieutenant Jerry Rawlings, the rank and file in the armed forces assumed state power in Ghana. Military revolts from the ranks, however, were not new in Africa. In 1964 mutinies had broken out in the East African countries of Kenya, Tanganyika and Uganda which were followed shortly afterwards by counter-coups organized by senior officers. In Sierra Leone in 1968 the country was handed over to a civilian government by non-commissioned officers after their brief period in power. And this is what happened in Ghana in 1979; power was returned to a constitutionally elected government within a few months. It would appear that when the rank and file in the army take over in Africa, military rule is generally a short-lived affair.

Yet the coup in Ghana in 1979 was different from most coups. It was imbued with a strong moral ideology and moral fervour. The revolt was a military uprising against previous corrupt (military) governments. '4 June is not a coup, it's an uprising', Rawlings proclaimed. The prime aim of 4 June was that of 'house-cleaning'; to declare war on dishonesty, especially in high places. It comprised within itself a demand for a moral revolution. And when the military rulers believed that their objective had been attained (consequent upon the execution of eight top civilian and military leaders, including two former heads of state, and the various attacks on 'kalabule', or corruption and inefficiency), they agreed to return to constitutional government.[38] Yet within fifteen months, on 31 December 1981, Rawlings had assumed power again.

Once again the revolt was from the rank and file of Ghana's military forces. But this time the military rulers went beyond the desire to oust corruption to inquire why Ghana was corrupt. The coup of 31 December addressed itself to more fundamental questions. In his first broadcast, Rawlings declared that the seizure of power was 'not a coup. I ask for nothing less than a revolution, something that will transform the social and economic order of this country.'[39] Corruption would clearly not disappear through moral exhortation and preaching and punishment of offenders. Its causes were deep-seated and complex and not unrelated to the social relations of neo-colonialism. The new military leaders concluded that the various ills afflicting Ghana required a major restructuring of society and economy. Fundamental changes will have to be achieved, changes that go well beyond a mere high-minded, house-cleaning exercise. In a country such as Ethiopia revolutionary changes have accompanied military rule. Such changes have been associated with wider mass struggle. In Ghana since 1982 military revolt from the ranks has begun to be linked with the cause of the workers and peasants. The talk is now of a 'People's Revolution' or 'People's Ghana'. Although still in its early and tentative stage, a movement to achieve a general democratization of Ghanaian society has commenced. People's Defence Committees, reflecting new popular institutions, have been formed throughout the country, and it is hoped that they will serve as the basis for general social transformation. Whether revolutionary developments will in fact occur, remains to be seen.[40] The main, initial problem, however, would appear to be the very survival of the military regime itself. At least four abortive coups – initiated by 'middle class' elements (such as businessmen, professionals, ex-politicians, and senior army officers) – were reported in Ghana between late 1982 and mid-1983. Counter-revolutionary forces are not to be so easily ousted from power and privilege and if the regime is to survive to attempt a wholesale recasting of economy and society it will have to ensure (as it is seeking to do) its popular support among the workers and peasants to withstand the strong and determined middle-class challenge.

NOTES

1 For a general and introductory discussion of classes in Africa, see Robin Cohen, 'Class in Africa: Analytical Problems and Perspectives', in Ralph

Miliband and John Saville (eds.), *The Socialist Register 1972* (London, 1972), pp. 231–55.

2 See for example, Fred M. Hayward, 'Rural Attitudes and Expectations about National Government: Experiences in Selected Ghanaian Communities', *Rural Africana*, No. 18 (1972), pp. 40–59.

3 Piet Konings, 'Political Consciousness and Political Action of Industrial Workers in Ghana: A Case Study of Valco Workers at Tema', *African Perspectives*, 2 (1978), p. 78.

4 See the discussion in Jim Silver, 'Class Struggles in Ghana's Mining Industry', *Review of African Political Economy*, No. 12 (1978), pp. 79–83, on covert forms of workplace struggle.

5 This distinction is derived, in large part, from Peter Waterman, 'Workers in the Third World', *Monthly Review*, 29, 4 (1977), pp. 59–64.

6 All quotations in this paragraph are from Richard Jeffries, *Class, Power and Ideology in Ghana: The Railwaymen of Sekondi-Takoradi* (Cambridge, 1978), pp. 99, 73, 96.

7 See Giovanni Arrighi and John S. Saul, *Essays on the Political Economy of Africa* (New York, 1973), pp. 44–102, 105–51. See also John S. Saul, 'The "Labour Aristocracy" Thesis Reconsidered', in Richard Sandbrook and Robin Cohen (eds.), *The Development of an African Working Class: Studies in Class Formation and Action* (London, 1975), pp. 303–10.

8 For a refutation of this thesis, see Richard Sandbrook, 'The Political Potential of African Urban Workers', *Canadian Journal of African Studies*, 11, 3 (1977), pp. 413–23; Richard Sandbrook, *The Politics of Basic Needs. Urban Aspects of Assaulting Poverty in Africa* (London, 1982), pp. 128–37.

9 For Zambian examples, see, for instance, Robert H. Bates, *Unions, Parties, and Political Development. A study of Mineworkers in Zambia* (New Haven, 1971), pp. 112–14; Philip Daniel, *Africanisation, Nationalisation and Inequality. Mining Labour and the Copperbelt in Zambian Development* (Cambridge, 1979), pp. 40–1, 80.

10 Adrian J. Peace, *Choice, Class and Conflict. A study of Southern Nigerian Factory Workers* (Brighton, 1979), pp. 174–6; and 'The Lagos Proletariat: Labour Aristocrats or Populist Militants?' in Sandbrook and Cohen, op. cit., pp. 281–302.

11 Frantz Fanon, *The Wretched of the Earth* (Harmondsworth, 1967).

12 Gavin Williams, 'Political Consciousness among the Ibadan Poor', in Emanuel de Kadt and Gavin Williams (eds.), *Sociology and Development* (London, 1974), pp. 109–22. For a slightly more detailed discussion of non-wage-earners, see Sandbrook, *The Politics of Basic Needs*, op. cit., pp. 156–68, 170–2.

13 Basil Davidson, 'African Peasants and Revolution', *Journal of Peasant Studies*, 1, 3 (1974), pp. 269–90.

14 The arguments developed here are derived, in the main, from John S. Saul, 'African Peasants and Revolution', *Review of African Political Economy*, No. 1 (1974), pp. 42–52.

15 See, for example, Roger Tangri, 'Conflict and Violence in Contemporary Sierra Leone Chiefdoms', *Journal of Modern African Studies*, 14, 2 (1976), pp. 311–21.

16   For a slightly more detailed discussion, see Robert H. Bates, *Markets and States in Tropical Africa. The Political Basis of Agricultural Policies* (Berkeley, 1981), Chap. 7. The quotation is from p. 118.

17   Michael G. Schatzberg, *Politics and Class in Zaire. Bureaucracy, Business and Beer in Lisala* (New York, 1980), p. 59.

18   See Donal B. Cruise O'Brien, 'Ruling Class and Peasantry in Senegal, 1960–1976: The Politics of a Monocrop Economy', in Rita Cruise O'Brien (ed.), *The Political Economy of Underdevelopment. Dependence in Senegal* (Beverly Hills, 1979), pp. 209–27. The quotations are from pp. 221, 222, 223–4.

19   Samuel Decalo, 'Regionalism, Political Decay, and Civil Strife in Chad', *Journal of Modern African Studies*, 18, 1 (1980), pp. 39–40.

20   Renée C. Fox, Willy de Craemer and Jean-Marie Ribeaucourt, 'The "Second Independence": A Case Study of the Kwilu Rebellion in the Congo', *Comparative Studies in Society and History*, 8, 1 (1965), pp. 78, 99.

21   Christopher E. F. Beer and Gavin Williams, 'The Politics of the Ibadan Peasantry', *The African Review*, 5, 3 (1975), p. 247.

22   For the Agbekoya rebellions of 1968–9 see also Christopher Beer, *The Politics of Peasant Groups in Western Nigeria* (Ibadan, 1976), Chaps. 7 and 8.

23   This concluding discussion is based on Beer and Williams, op. cit., especially p. 255.

24   Nelson Kasfir, *The Shrinking Political Arena. Participation and Ethnicity in African Politics with a Case Study of Uganda* (Berkeley, 1976), Chap. 5 describes the politics of ethnic involvement in Uganda.

25   For a recent summary discussion, see Larry Diamond, 'Class, Ethnicity, and the Democratic State: Nigeria, 1950–1966', *Comparative Studies in Society and History*, 25, 3 (1983), pp. 457–89.

26   My discussion in this section is based, in the main, on Morris Szeftel, *Conflict, Spoils and Class Formation in Zambia* (University of Manchester, Ph.D., 1978); Carolyn L. Baylies and Morris Szeftel, 'The Rise of a Zambian Capitalist Class in the 1970s', *Journal of Southern African Studies*, 8, 2 (1982) pp. 187–213; and Segun Osoba, 'The Nigerian Power Elite, 1952–65', in Peter C. W. Gutkind and Peter Waterman (eds.), *African Social Studies. A Radical Reader* (London, 1977), pp. 368–82. For a discussion of the political dynamics of class formation in rural Zaire, see Schatzberg, op. cit., *passim*.

27   This discussion is based on Carolyn L. Baylies, *The State and Class Formation in Zambia* (University of Wisconsin, Ph.D., 1978).

28   Alan B. Amey and David K. Leonard, 'Public Policy, Class and Inequality in Kenya and Tanzania', *Africa Today*, 26, 4 (1979). The quotation is from p. 22 while the discussion is on pp. 19–22.

29   Claude Meillassoux, 'A Class Analysis of the Bureaucratic Process in Mali', *Journal of Development Studies*, 6, 2 (1970), p. 106.

30   Gavin Williams and Terisa Turner, 'Nigeria', in John Dunn (ed.), *West African States. Failure and Promise* (Cambridge, 1978), p. 157.

31   Szeftel, op. cit., p. 439. The same argument is to be found in Baylies and Szeftel, op. cit., pp. 205–9, and in Karen Eriksen, 'Zambia: Class Formation and Detente', *Review of African Political Economy*, No. 9 (1978), pp. 18–26.

32   Segun Osoba, 'The Deepening Crisis of the Nigerian National Bourgeoisie',

Review of African Political Economy, No. 13 (1978), p. 72.

33   Nicola Swainson, *The Development of Corporate Capitalism in Kenya 1918–77* (London, 1980), p. 187. For a more detailed discussion of this case as well as of another similar case, see pp. 187–9, 190–1. For the Zambian experience, see Baylies and Szeftel, op. cit., pp. 209–11.

34   Colin Leys, 'Development Strategy in Kenya since 1971', *Canadian Journal of African Studies*, 13, 1/2 (1979), p. 303.

35   John S. Saul, 'The State in Post-Colonial Societies: Tanzania', in Ralph Miliband and John Saville (eds.), *The Socialist Register 1974* (London, 1974), pp. 358, 363–4.

36   See Schatzberg, op. cit., pp. 161–4. The quotation is from p. 163.

37   Ralph Miliband, *The State in Capitalist Society. The Analysis of the Western System of Power* (London, 1973), p. 67.

38   A number of arguments contained in this section of the chapter are derived from Jan Pieterse, 'Rawlings and the 1979 revolt in Ghana', *Race and Class*, 23, 4 (1982), pp. 251–73.

39   Quoted in Victoria Brittain, 'Ghana's Precarious Revolution', *New Left Review*, No. 140 (1983), p. 50.

40   See Kwarteng Mensah, 'The December intervention and the current situation in Ghana', *Race and Class*, 24, 1 (1982), pp. 71–8; and Brittain, op. cit., for recent discussions.

Political Control, Participation and Institutionalization

5

Political control

As argued in Chapter 2, politicians in independent Africa have sought to attain power primarily because of the advantages (for some the riches) associated with political office; and once in office they have been anxious to maintain themselves in power and have, to this end, employed various means to ensure their hegemony. Related to this is the fact that, as discussed in Chapter 3, state personnel create the conditions for economic production to take place and in the process further their own appropriation. But, in addition, as this present chapter shows, the power-holders are obliged to establish the political conditions for the benefits of political power to be acquired and enhanced. Conditions such as the management of conflict and the promotion of internal order and stability are often proclaimed as being in the interest of the whole population but are, in the main, more conducive to the interest of the ruling group. Thus, for example, for capital accumulation (either on the part of state personnel or the emergent indigenous bourgeoisie or both) to proceed without major difficulties, the state has to contain conflict and ensure a modicum of order. For the power-holders the conditions requisite for the maintenance and enlargement of their power and privileges have required the control of the political process. And the most common political mechanism for the exercise of such control has been authoritarian government.

A tendency towards authoritarian rule was prevalent among the political leaders who assumed state power at the time of political independence. The political culture of the new leadership predisposed it to take 'a proprietary view of governmental authority'. The colonial regime itself had been highly authoritarian (the colonial state in the Congo was colloquially known as 'Bula Matari' – crusher of rocks) and had been the only governmental system of which the African politicians had had any actual experience. The constitutional and democratic system devised for the new political leaders by the departing colonialists did not have deep roots. Moreover, the nationalist movements had sought to unite the people against colonial rule: those who now opposed the independence government were, not surprisingly, seen as being disloyal.

These factors were reinforced by powerful considerations of self-interest: political leaders wanted to make themselves secure in the enjoyment of the lucrative rewards of politics. What Pratt writes in regard to Tanzania has a wider relevance in sub-Saharan Africa.

> The political leaders of TANU had, after all, won independence for Tanzania. They had, themselves, long been without secure employment or regular incomes. They had now become the inheritors of the colonial regime. Political office was very likely the only way in which many of them were able to earn a significant income. Few had professional or technical skills which would have made them easily employable within the government service and there was no large private sector capable of absorbing them in any number. For many, therefore, a loss of political office would have meant an eventual return to peasant farming. It is small wonder that many TANU leaders tended to jump rather swiftly to the view that critics of TANU ought to be restrained.[1]

These tendencies towards authoritarianism have been intensified in much of Africa by the continuing economic difficulties experienced in most countries. Serious economic and administrative failure of state personnel coupled with their corruption and self-enrichment have alienated them increasingly from the mass of the people. Whatever popular legitimacy African governments enjoyed at the time of independence has declined. Mounting mass economic discontent and distrust of political and administrative leaders has forced the latter to turn themselves into an authoritarian oligarchy relying more and more on coercion to keep themselves in power.

Whether under civilian or military leadership, the direction in sub-Saharan Africa since independence has been decidedly authoritarian.[2] The authoritarian trends typical of independent Africa have included the conferment of sweeping powers on the presidential executive and canonization of the almighty leaders; the declining importance of the legislature and the weakening of legislative authority;[3] the dismantling of other elected institutions, such as local government authorities, and their replacement by bureaucrats and self-appointed politicians; the manipulation or abolition of elections; the disbanding of opposition parties and the institution of single-party systems; and the control by the state or governing party of autonomous trade unions, co-operatives, newspapers and broadcast media. In their quest to maintain control over the political process, governments all over the African continent have resorted to the same array of measures although, as we shall see, the authoritarian hand has been lighter in some than others. Yet the trend towards more or less pronounced forms of authoritarian government in sub-Saharan Africa has been clear. Hardly any African regime has brooked any bounds to its rule. In Apter's vivid terms: 'the billiard game of politics is being played on a table that constantly grows smaller'.[4]

The personalistic nature of government and the concentration of power in the presidential executive are features characteristic of the political process in most African countries. Most rulers have attained a personal ascendancy over the political system and Africa has succumbed, to an important extent, to personal rule.[5] Writing in the early 1960s, Austin declared that Kwame Nkrumah of Ghana was 'more than ready to fit the role of an African Tsar'[6] and it is clear that hardly any African leader has sought to check the movement towards personal rule. The aggregation of personal power can be exemplified by the case of Zaire, where Mobutu Sese Seko has headed the ruling party, the MPR, and has presided over the Council of Ministers, the legislature and Supreme Judicial Council as well as the Party Political Bureau. 'In effect,' writes Young, 'the members of all those bodies were named by the President, whose words and thoughts cumulatively constituted the official doctrine of the country (Mobutisme), and had the force of law.'[7]

Elections on a competitive basis in contemporary black Africa have been conspicuous by their general absence. Competitive elections among rival political parties have hardly been held. Where they have been held, mainly in the early independence years, they were marked by electoral falsifications and irregularities. In the case of competitive elections that have taken place within the framework of the one-party state, as has occurred in a few countries, the electoral rules have 'made it clear that the voter was not being offered the choice of a government' but that the elections had as their prime purpose the 'renewal of the personnel of the parliamentary elite'.[8] Elsewhere in much of Africa, elections have merely meant voters approving official candidates. In some countries, the view that the people's representatives should be selected by the people has been totally abandoned: in Ghana in 1965, for example, a whole parliament of 198 members was hand-picked by the Central Committee of the CPP and returned unopposed.

Shortly after independence there was a widespread trend towards single-party systems. The public existence of opposition parties was suppressed by ruling parties. But within a few years it was evident that the trend was towards the emergence of no-party systems, that is, states in which the state bureaucracy was acquiring unrivalled power whilst political parties were declining as institutional sources of authority. Throughout Africa the dominant party's organization and functions have undergone a process of 'inanition'; parties are seldom more than bureaucratic shells.[9] The independence period has seen nearly everywhere the progressive bureacratization of the state and mounting concentration of administrative responsibility in the hands of senior state personnel. Central government bureaucracies have been enlarged (with public administration consuming ever greater proportions of government expenditures); have increased in power (at the expense of popularly elected institutions such as local government authorities); and have asserted increasing control over autonomous trade unions, co-operatives and the mass media. The process of administrative centralization has been particularly pronounced in military regimes which have removed participatory structures (such as elections and parties) and worked closely with the civilian bureaucracy.

That most governments have been authoritarian and have often resorted to coercion and suppression to maintain political domination is widely acknowledged. As seen in Chapter 2, incumbent regimes have hindered opposition politicians and prevented them from organizing themselves for competition and struggle. At the same time, the ordinary citizen has been denied the right to participate fully in decision-making and has, moreover, suffered from lack of liberty and the stifling of civil freedoms. Limited or minimal political involvement by the populace[10] has resulted in many an African state losing the loyalty of a substantial proportion of its population. Political legitimacy has been low; and it has not been sufficient to guarantee the long-term survival of Africa's governments.

Africa's regimes have proved notoriously precarious. Few have succeeded in ensuring order and stability, and conflict and challenge have been inadequately contained. Many have been toppled, often with relative facility, and most have been plagued by a succession of plots, reprisals and attempts at assassination (fomented by elite political competitors), by strikes, demonstrations and revolts (organized by workers and peasants). Although the downfall of Africa's civilian and military regimes has, as argued in Chapter 2, been the result of elite conflict, it has been precipitated by their marked lack of political legitimacy in the eyes of the mass of the people.

Political participation

The issue of legitimacy is not one that Africa's rulers have been oblivious to. The value of legitimacy is that a legitimate regime need not maintain itself primarily by force. History, too, suggests that governments founded on force are unstable and short-lived. Africa's rulers, whether civilians or soldiers, have realized that legitimacy rather than coercion should be the preferred basis of supremacy if they are to retain political power. Thus, especially in recent years, they have striven to establish consent and legitimacy to enhance their political security.

The fostering of 'intra-elite' cohesion has been seen as crucial to the operation of a stable and legitimate system of rule. Given the fact that Africa's regimes have rarely been toppled consequent upon direct mass political action, the continued existence of a government has been largely based on the establishment of support of a country's leaders. Governments have adopted various stratagems to secure such support. One has been the adoption of patron–client structures. For example, the political dominance achieved by the governing party in Senegal derives in large part from the alliances which national party leaders have skilfully maintained, since the early 1950s, with the most important traditional and religious authorities in rural society. The marabouts and other locally powerful 'clan' politicians constituted an important pillar of the Senghor regime.[11] In Sierra Leone, on the other hand, the ruling APC has sought to further its security and legitimacy by incorporating opposition SLPP politicians within the government. By offering opposition members political office, ruling parties throughout Africa have hoped to build a broader leadership coalition more likely to legitimate the hegemony of the ruling group.

Ruling groups have also begun to create political institutions which are capable of providing a stable base of popular support for the government and consequently a basis for more durable rule. Some form of popular approval has been recognized as necessary for generating legitimacy and various structures have been set up to mobilize mass support. The quest for a popular mandate has usually been sought by means of elections, but various formal mechanisms have been instituted to achieve legitimation of the state. Many of these participatory devices (involving the participation of the people in politics) will be considered subsequently. Here it is important to note that African regimes have attempted to evoke support through increasing citizen participation in the political system.

In addition, governments have sought to inculcate commitments to the national authority and constitutional arrangements. Through the diffusion of official ideologies, for example, an attempt has been made to elicit the suport of the people for the political system. Certainly there has been no dearth of official ideologies in independent Africa: 'Nkrumaism' (Ghana), 'Humanism' (Zambia), 'Mobutisme' (Zaire), 'Nyayoism' (Kenya) and so on. These official ideologies have typically stressed similar themes, such as those of classlessness and national unity. Conflict between classes is declared not to exist or, where it does, such conflict must be dissipated. All are exhorted to 'pull together' in the combined interests of the nation under the guidance and direction of the ruling party. But such ideologies would appear not to have had much impact in legitimating the existing political order. The precepts and principles contained in the various ideologies have not been inculcated by the majority of the population and nor have the ideologies proven successful in buttressing the hegemony of rulers.[12]

In examining the various mechanisms that have been set up to enhance political legitimacy through increasing popular participation, it has to be observed that governments have embodied more of the elements of control than they have of democratic participation, which has often been the avowed justification for their existence. Control and participation have gone hand in hand as a means of maintaining political domination and developing political legitimacy. Control from above has accompanied citizen participation partly to ensure that participation takes place within a framework conducive to the preservation of national unity but mainly, it would appear, to preserve the interests of the leadership in power and ensure that the ruling group is not threatened, although particular individuals may lose their positions. Political participation in independent Africa has generally been limited to providing the ruling group with a semblance of popular approval without in any important way threatening the political domination of that group. One recent example may be cited here of the sort of balance being struck between participation and control. Under President Senghor, Senegal instituted in the late 1970s constitutional reforms whereby a competitive multi-party system was inaugurated. A constitutional amendment of 1976 provided for legal recognition of new political parties with assigned positions along a left-right ideological spectrum. But the rival parties to the governing Parti Socialiste Sénégalais (PS) were carefully selected and the re-emergence of approved parties did not ensure that freedom was afforded to truly threatening groups, in particular to Cheik Anta Diop's Rassemblement National Démocratique, arguably the party at the time with the widest popular support after the ruling PS. Senghor's party further allocated to itself what was generally acknowledged as the most widely appealing party label – 'socialist and democratic' – which was also desired by rival parties; the remaining labels of 'liberal and democratic' and 'Marxist-Leninist or Communist' appear to have been rather reluctantly accepted by other parties wishing to enter the political arena. These changes did not threaten the dominant position of the PS. In the legislative elections of 1978 the PS won 83 of the national assembly's 100 seats. The exclusion of rival parties from electoral competition together with the fact that those included were handicapped by the system of official labels, resulted in the PS being scarcely threatened with displacement, at least by electoral means.

It is widely accepted that nearly all sub-Saharan African states have evolved towards forms of authoritarianism. But within the broad outline the situation has varied, often considerably, from country to country. Although nearly all of these regimes display many characteristics common to authoritarian rule, some are more authoritarian than others. However controlled or limited popular participation in politics may be, there are some countries where popular involvement does exist. Three types of regimes may be distinguished according to the balance between political control and political participation.[13]

The first type of regime that can be distinguished is the one where the extent of authoritarian rule is at its greatest. Such regimes are typically military ones, where the usual pattern is for societies to be depoliticized with the state itself assuming a monopoly of political activity. The military generally, although (as indicated below) not always, rules without holding elections. There is therefore no use of elections to provide the basis for support for the military government as is the case with civilian regimes. Moreoever, political parties are banned and all other political and parapolitical associations strictly controlled. In abolishing such organizations, the military create a vacuum between themselves and the people. To provide a link with the people the military has perforce to rely on the civil service. At times the military bring civilians into their administration but, nevertheless, a close relationship is formed between soldiers and bureaucrats in the management of the polity. This relationship results in a greater centralization of political power. As a result, military regimes place greater reliance on force and the popularity of their policies in order to maintain themselves in power.

Within this category also fall Africa's repressive regimes which have hardly permitted any popular participation. Uganda under Amin, the Central African Republic under Bokassa, and Equatorial Guinea under Nguema were all regimes under dictators which were less inhibited in resorting to force and coercion to curtail participation and intimidate opposition. All of them witnessed a wholesale dismantling of all democratic institutions and the total subversion of all liberties.[14] Such was the rule of terror under Nguema that it was estimated that by the late 1970s one-third of the population (around 100 000) persons) lived in exile. But all of these autocratic regimes have been eventually overthrown, attesting to the argument that force alone cannot sustain repressive regimes for long and act as an ultimate substitute for legitimation.

(g) The second type – plebiscitory one-party regimes – are found mostly in ex-French Africa but also elsewhere on the continent and include military governments which have 'politicized' their rule (for example, by founding political parties) such as those in Zaire and Benin. Such regimes provide very limited opportunities for participation except, periodically, at elections. Governments make a major effort to use elections to mobilize popular support for those in power. Although the outcome of these elections is not in doubt, they provide an occasion for the symbolic ratification of government policy and personages. The voters are presented with only one list and can vote only for or against official candidates. Official returns for these elections report exceptionally high levels of affirmative voting and turnout. In Zaire in 1970 the approved candidates received an overwhelming majority (98.33 per cent) of all the votes cast in the parliamentary elections. In 1978 in the Cameroun Federal Republic, following the expiry of the National Assembly's term of office, 3 614 768 of the 3 615 463 votes cast approved the single list of candidates for election presented by the ruling Union Nationale Camerounaise. Similarly in Guinea in 1980, out of 2.5 million voters, 2.4 million officially registered their approval of the single list of candidates presented to the electorate by the Parti Démocratique de Guinée. But what is important about these elections does not lie in the accuracy of official returns but in the extent to which the election constitutes a symbol or myth of the legitimacy of the government. Doubtless there is substantial over-reporting of the official figures; yet, sizeable numbers of people are, in fact, mobilized in a ritual and passive act of voting for approved candidates. The citizens are mobilized in an attempt to ratify, through the show of mass support in elections, the government, its policies and its personnel. The purpose is thus to provide the ruling group with a semblance of popular approval as well as to enhance its legitimacy.

Other modes and structures of participation are, however, minimal: in between elections public participation in politics is severely restricted. Although at times measures have been proclaimed to enhance citizen participation, little has been done to implement them. The ruled are very much subjects, not citizens in countries such as Benin and Zaire. In Benin in late 1973 the government arrived at a formula for the 'decentralization' of the administration that would permit 'the organized masses to recover control of the state apparatus'. But the new structures were soon moribund. The idea of a legitimizing proletarian party was also accepted but, as Decalo observes, the Benin People's Revolutionary Party was born 'under tight military control in May 1976'.[15] Indeed, parties in all such regimes have hardly served as mobilizing agencies – mobilizing people to the goals expressed in party manifestos; rather they have been mechanisms for undermining or co-opting opposition elements, for distributing patronage, and for eliciting support for the ruling group. 'In essence,' comments one writer of the ruling party in Zaire, 'the Mouvement populaire de la revolution is the propaganda arm of the state and not really a political party at all.'[16]

The third type of regime – the competitive one-party regime – is more ③ typical of a number of ex-British African countries, although it has also begun to be adopted in some francophone African countries such as the Ivory Coast. The pattern of elections is different in this case. Here some electoral choice exists although it is restricted to candidates approved by the governing party. Yet the threat of former parliamentarians losing their seats is not an entirely unreal one. In the 1975 elections in Tanzania, 43 MPs were not returned and two ministers failed to be re-elected. In the 1979 general elections in Kenya, 72 out of a total of 158 fifteen assistant ministers. In the 1980 elections in the Ivory Coast, of the 80 incumbent Deputies who ran for re-election only 27 were returned. Moreover, not so much emphasis is placed by the government on attaining high levels of electoral participation. As Collier observes: 'Legitimacy in these regimes derives more from popular choice, however limited or controlled it may be, than it does from the ritual of mass ratification'.[17] Moreover, other kinds of participation are encouraged in the urban and rural areas. But the involvement of the citizenry has not been unlimited and, as our following case-studies seek to show, many if not all of these institutions have proven to be much more of control mechanisms for the central authority rather than fully-fledged agencies for grass-roots participation.

The tension between participation and control in this third type of regime may be examined in regard to three countries – Tanzania, Zambia and Mozambique – where the idea of entrusting 'power to the people' and creating 'participatory democracy' has been constantly articulated since independence. In Tanzania and Zambia, various attempts have been made to enhance citizen participation. Both have, for instance, devised similar systems of elections within their one-party polities; instituted measures to decentralize the government; and set up a series of workplace institutions to ensure worker participation. But in both countries these have turned out to be largely hollow structures. Elections are strictly controlled affairs: the number of candidates in each constituency is limited to two (in Tanzania) and three (in Zambia) and all candidates are carefully screened by the party before being permitted to stand for election.[18] Decentralization has taken the form of administrative deconcentration, entailing the delegation of authority from central government ministries to field officers. Elected local government authorities have also declined in importance and autonomy, being dominated by the administrative and technical officials.[19] Workers' committees and councils have also not stimulated much participation and industrial democracy; they have been largely dominated by management.[20] In addition, other representative institutions have declined in importance. The legislature has had its power reduced;[21] the independence of trade unions has been whittled away and trade-union rights, notably the right to strike, have been surrounded by more stringent inhibitions. By the standards of parties elsewhere on the African continent, TANU (since 1977 known as CCM) and, to a lesser extent, UNIP have been parties of some ideological and organizational strength. But they have been far from the monolithic organizations they have sometimes been portrayed as and have been weak in mobilizing the people. Moreover, the expansion of the party bureaucracy into the localities has occurred simultaneously with the growth of decentralized state personnel, thus leading to the build-up of an ever-larger bureaucratic presence.[22] Indeed, in both countries the proportion of government expenditures devoted to bureaucracy has become progressively larger; in the 1970s Tanzania's public administration grew by over 10 per cent a year and almost doubled (92 per cent increase) between 1972 and 1979. To be sure both countries have incorporated a number of democratic features in their political systems; and there is no denying that Tanzanians and Zambians have the opportunity to exert much more political influence and pressure than most other peoples in sub-Saharan Africa. But those in control of the state have also been able to contain and reduce popular influence and pressure within the political system.

Writing about Tanzania, Saul notes 'the ultimate preemption of anything like a real and radical democratization of the system there';[23] while in Mozambique democracy is 'quite tangible' and 'indeed, it is more than impressive'.[24] The idea of popular participation ('people's power') and, in particular, the explicit rejection of 'commandism' is given repeated emphasis in the statements of the Mozambican political leadership. This emphasis 'probably resulted from Frelimo's experiences during the war of national liberation, when it required the support of the population and had only a limited number of cadres to organize and mobilize the people. Rejection of commandism was as much a necessity as an ideological choice.'[25]

In spite of all the stress on the establishment of a decentralized and participatory democracy, in the view of many reality has not matched rhetoric. The tension between state direction and popular power has persisted. To examine the nature of this tension we need to look at the major institutions set up to ensure popular participation – the party, the 'dynamizing groups', the mass organizations, and the people's assemblies. The party and the dynamizing groups ('grupo dynamizadorc') are closely related and need to be considered together. Frelimo has relied to some extent on the dynamizing groups to mobilize the population. The dynamizing groups were introduced during the transitional government period (1974–5) in central and southern Mozambique (where Frelimo had little influence) and became one of the key vehicles for direct contact between the party organizers and the mass of unorganized people. Hundreds of dynamizing groups were established in places of residence, work and study, as well as in government bureaucracies. Of special importance was the fact that they were not organized from the top down; the members were popularly elected and they were therefore not pure party cells or part of a bureaucratic structure.[26] But at its Third Congress in 1977, Frelimo proclaimed itself to be a Marxist–Leninist 'Vanguard Party of the Socialist Revolution' and no longer a mass movement; membership was limited and the criteria for membership considerably tightened. As for the dynamizing groups, the Ottaways argue that

> the very logic of the vanguard party appeared such as to doom them to disappear, or at least change completely in character . . . By 1979, a consensus seemed to have emerged that the groups would disappear in the rural areas as soon as a Frelimo cell was implanted but would continue to exist in urban areas as neighbourhood committees, dealing primarily with concrete problems and not with general political issues. [27]

As the dynamizing groups declined in importance, the major avenue for political participation open to those members of the population who were not members of Frelimo – the large majority – was the mass organizations of women, youth and labour. The Ottaways state, however, that 'the mass organizations were subordinated to and controlled by the Party' and that, by and large, they 'all saw their task as that of mobilizing their respective constituencies to help implement party policies'.[28] Saul is full of praise for Frelimo although not unaware of the benevolent control exercised by the party:

> It is true that the party plays a crucial part, itself screening candidates, for example, and, in the case of the selection of party members, taking the role of popular scrutiny as being merely advisory to it. The parameters of participation continue to be defined, in part, from the top down, this reality representing, in the eyes of Frelimo leaders, precisely the measure of leadership and guidance of the development process necessitated by the present situation.

Yet, at the same time,

> the various meetings and elections . . . are scarcely formalities: inputs at the base are vital, they do reach the top, and, as so many activists themselves testified, they create a situation in which party and administrative functionaries must become cadres capable of realising their goals by political and educational means, rather than by administrative fiat, or be seen to fail. Indeed, a stage seems to have been reached where the assertions of workers and peasants which these structures have actively elicited can be ignored only at the regime's peril.[29]

Although also sympathetic to the political system being set up in Mozambique, others are more critical of how the organs of popular participation relate to the vanguard party, Frelimo, and see the masses being involved essentially as objects of mobilization rather than as creative participants. For instance, the elections held in late 1977 to elect 'people's assemblies' at the local, district, municipal, provincial and national levels varied in their democratic content. At the local level the elections 'were a particularly striking example of grassroots democracy at work';[30] but the higher-level assemblies were elected indirectly and the members of the National People's Assembly 'were simply chosen by Frelimo's Central Committee and the list submitted to the provincial bodies for *pro forma* ratification'.[31]

Since then the weakness of the party in the rural areas, consequent upon the shortage of skilled middle-level cadres, has become widely recognized. The following comment by the Secretary of the Ideological Committee of the party reflects the relationship between party cadres and the masses.

> The sector for party ideological work has now closed in on itself. It is not directed towards the masses. It is isolated from the people. It is a sector that functions essentially for itself and by itself and not for the masses. It is a sector where, at present, the central practice is not so much political mobilization and ideological education of the people, but the holding of meetings and seminars.

There are few meetings with the masses, especially in the rural areas. Moreover, the few meetings that they hold are often meetings in which the party member arrives, talks and goes away. They are not meetings to hear from the people about their problems. They are meetings in which the people only participate as listeners and observers.

The result 'is that the people do not participate effectively in making decisions, and do not carry through on decisions made'.[32]

In a system such as that in Mozambique, where there has been a simultaneous emphasis on 'centralism' and 'democracy', or on 'people's power' and the rule of a 'vanguard party', a serious dilemma is liable to occur. And it is this dilemma that has given rise to conflicting interpretations, such as between those stressing participatory democracy and others emphasizing the greater authoritarianism of a vanguard party. Although in the view of various writers 'the forces favouring centralism seem to be winning out',[33] the population does have some say, especially about local problems and issues.

Political institutionalization

The pursuit of political legitimacy is not to be equated with political institutionalization. The latter is concerned with constitutionalism and questions relating, for example, to the limits on the exercise of power and the legitimate powers of government. The essence of political institutionalization is the introduction of rules and procedures so that political conduct is governed increasingly by them rather than by considerations of personal power. In contemporary sub-Saharan Africa, the acceptance of and abidance by constitutional rules has been partial and limited. Yet political institutionalization has been occurring in African states in recent years. The desire for a more settled kind of national politics consequent upon institutional rules has become gradually more evident. Two modes of political institutionalization may be distinguished: one is through major constitutional change, the other is by piecemeal constitutional reforms.[34]

New constitutions have been drawn up in several African countries, particularly those in which the military has withdrawn from positions of political power and government has been transferred to civilian rulers. Civilian governments have been installed after being elected under a new constitution in Ghana (1979), Nigeria (1979), and Upper Volta (1978). Constitutional issues have arisen the moment soldiers have accepted the need to restore civilian government; such restorations have raised questions about who should rule and how this was to be fairly determined. Acts of reconstitution have also been concerned to resolve basic political problems which have occurred in the past and which, it is hoped, can be prevented from recurring in the future. Constitutional measures have been devised to tackle 'intra-elite' competition and its accompanying problems such as those of ethnic conflict.

Nigeria's second independence constitution attempted to regulate political parties by defining strictly the conditions under which they were to be permitted to be organized and to function; parties were 'to reflect the federal character of Nigeria' and thus, for instance, their programmes had to be national in character and their executives national in composition. The constitutional provisions for winning the election for president likewise demanded that a candidate receive a plurality plus at least a quarter of the votes in two-thirds of the states. Through such measures it was hoped that the ethnic and regional basis of party competition that afflicted the first Nigerian Republic would be overcome, and thus the disorder and violent confrontation that was so much a part of that regime's political history might be averted. The new constitution also sought to confront the issue of political office being regarded as an avenue to wealth and prestige. The drafters of the constitution stated that, in the past, those who 'wielded the power of the state' were 'preoccupied with power and its material perquisites'. So great was this preoccupation that 'political ideals as to how society can be organized and ruled to the best advantage of all hardly enter into the calculation'. To remedy these ills, constitutional provisions provided *inter alia* for a 'Code of Conduct', backed by a 'Code of Conduct Tribunal', 'to ensure that persons who are entrusted with public authority do not abuse their trust and enrich themselves or defraud the nation'.[35]

Incremental institutionalization is concerned with more limited political purposes yet, like wholesale constitutional engineering, it attempts to introduce impersonal rules which will supersede factional or personal power interests as the main arbiters of political conduct within the state. The manner in which succession of political office – especially that of the presidency – from one person to another is to take place is an example of such piecemeal institutionalization. The succession of President Moi to the Kenyan presidency following the death of President Kenyatta was an instance of a constitutional transfer of power. Peaceful and procedural transfer of power also occurred in Senegal after the retirement of President Senghor in December 1980, and reflects institutionalization rather than power politics. In both Kenya and Senegal the purpose of constitutional rules was to avert the personal and factional competition for office that had characterized the politics of these countries in the past. Indeed, the new constitutions as well as the more specific constitutional reforms were major attempts to regulate competition among politicians to ensure 'elite' cohesion of the ruling group and stability at the centre of the political system.

In Senegal, as well, partisan political activity has been introduced. As we have seen, Senghor experimented with a controlled three-party system but his successor, Abdou Diouf, permitted various parties to contest elections and the political system was opened to all comers (*politique d'ouverture*). In the February 1983 general election, eight parties participated. The governing party won 109 of the 120 seats in the assembly but two opposition parties also obtained representation. The introduction of a multi-party democracy in Senegal is another illustration of a new trend emerging in contemporary Africa to create stable and legitimate polities in which institutionalized conventions and procedures rather than power politics govern political conduct. A fourth type of regime may therefore be discerned: the multi-party regime. Only two countries, Botswana and the Gambia, have been able to sustain a multi-party system since independence (Botswana, for instance, held regular multi-party elections in 1969, 1974, 1979 and 1984). But with the re-adoption of multi-partyism in recent years in Nigeria (1979) and Senegal (1983) it is possible that a more democratic political development may be in the process of being inaugurated. Such a political development entails political institutions such as parties, legislatures and elections and through them the people playing a key role in resolving power conflicts and controlling power relations according to constitutional rules and procedures. Under such circumstances the institutionalization of a constitutional government (as opposed to an authoritarian one) is furthered and the rule of those in power determined according to more democratic processes.

The introduction of, and compliance with, rules and procedures is an essential first step towards the establishment of political order in contemporary Africa. Constitutional politics can foster the 'intra-elite' cohesion so necessary for political stability and thus alleviate the political turmoil that has characterized Africa since independence. But political institutionalization also rests on the legitimacy of popular consent. The new constitutions and constitutional rules have to be seen to be promoting the interests of the mass of the population and furthering mass involvement in the political sphere. The participation of the people is essential in securing popular control of government rather than, as in much of Africa, government control of the people through their involvement in the political process. So long as the new institutional rules are unable to legitimate the political system in the eyes of the people and merely perpetuate the domination of the ruling group (albeit regulating its political intrigues and political battles), then Africa's polities will continue to be high on the scale of disorder and autocracy and low in popular esteem and political stability. This is well exemplified in the overthrow of constitutional governments in Ghana (31 December 1982) and in Nigeria (31 December 1983). Although intra-elite competition among politicians and soldiers was evident, the back-drop to the coups was electoral fraud and, especially, massive corruption among state personnel, combined with seriously deteriorating economic standards for the majority of people. With the exception of a few multi-party states such as Botswana, most other African governments remain precariously based in popular esteem, mired in a 'swamp of personal interests and egoistic ambitions'[36] and obliged to rely on coercion to maintain themselves in power.

NOTES

1   Quotations from Cranford Pratt, *The Critical Phase in Tanzania 1945–1968. Nyerere and the Emergence of a Socialist Strategy* (Cambridge, 1976), p. 185.
2   Martin L. Kilson, 'Authoritarian and Single-Party Tendencies in African Politics', *World Politics,* 15, 2 (1963), pp. 262–94.
3   See, for example, Newell M. Stultz, 'Parliaments in Former British Black Africa', *Journal of Developing Areas*, 2, 4 (1968), pp. 479–93.
4   David E. Apter, 'Ghana', in James S. Coleman and Carl G. Rosberg, Jr. (eds.), *Political Parties and National Integration in Tropical Africa* (Berkeley, 1966), p. 314.
5   See, for example, Robert H. Jackson and Carl G. Rosberg, *Personal Rule in Black Africa. Prince, Autocrat, Prophet, Tyrant* (Berkeley, 1982).
6   Dennis Austin, *Politics in Ghana, 1946–1960* (London, 1964), p. 42.
7   Crawford Young, 'Zaire: The Unending Crisis', *Foreign Affairs*, 57, 1 (1978), p. 171.
8   Goran Hyden and Colin Leys, 'Elections and Politics in Single-Party Systems: the Case of Kenya and Tanzania', *British Journal of Political Science*, 2, 4 (1972), p. 416.
9   For an early study, see Immanuel Wallerstein, 'The Decline of the Party in Single-Party African States', in Joseph La Palombara and Myron Weiner (eds.), *Political Parties and Political Development* (Princeton, 1966), pp. 201–14.
10   See, for example, Nelson Kasfir, 'Departicipation and Political Development in Black African Politics', *Studies in Comparative International Development*, 9, 3 (1974), pp. 3–25.
11   See, for example, Donal B. Cruise O'Brien, *Saints and Politicians. Essays in the Organization of a Senegalese Peasant Society* (Cambridge, 1975).
12   For one case study, see Michael G. Schatzberg, 'Fidélité au Guide: the JMPR in Zairean Schools', *Journal of Modern African Studies*, 16, 3 (1978), pp. 417–31.
13   The discussion that follows is based, to some extent, on Ruth Berins Collier, *Regimes in Tropical Africa. Changing Forms of Supremacy, 1945–1975* (Berkeley, 1982), Chap. 5.
14   For a discussion of the 'militarization' of the state in Amin's Uganda, see Mahmood Mamdani, *Imperialism and Fascism in Uganda* (London, 1983), Chap. 4.
15   Samuel Decalo, 'Ideological Rhetoric and Scientific Socialism in Benin and Congo/Brazzaville', in Carl G. Rosberg and Thomas M. Callaghy (eds.),

Socialism in Sub-Saharan Africa. A New Assessment (Berkeley, 1979), pp. 240, 242.

16   Thomas M. Callaghy, 'State–Subject Communication in Zaire: Domination and the Concept of Domain Consensus', *Journal of Modern African Studies*, 18, 3 (1980), p. 472.

17   Ruth Berins Collier, 'Parties, Coups, and Authoritarian Rule. Patterns of Political Change in Tropical Africa', *Comparative Political Studies*, 11, 1 (1978), p. 77.

18   The Election Study Committee, University of Dar es Salaam, *Socialism and Participation. Tanzania's 1970 National Elections* (Dar es Salaam, 1974); and Carolyn Baylies and Morris Szeftel, 'Control and Participation in the One-Party State, as Demonstrated in the 1973 General Elections (Zambia)' (unpublished paper).

19   Diana Conyers, 'Decentralization for Regional Development: A Comparative Study of Tanzania, Zambia and Papua New Guinea', *Public Administration and Development*, 1, 2 (1981), pp. 107–20.

20   Henry Mapolu, 'The Organization and Participation of Workers in Tanzania', *The African Review*, 2, 3 (1972), pp. 381–415; and Robin Fincham and Grace Zulu, 'Works Councils in Zambia. The Implementation of Industrial Participatory Democracy', *Labour and Society*, 5, 2 (1980), pp. 171–90.

21   William Tordoff, 'Residual Legislatures: The Cases of Tanzania and Zambia', *Journal of Commonwealth and Comparative Politics*, 15, 3 (1977), pp. 235–49.

22   Helge Kjekshus (ed.), *The Party. Essays on TANU* (Dar es Salaam); and Ian Scott, 'Party and Administration Under the One-Party State', in William Tordoff (ed.), *Administration in Zambia* (Manchester, 1980) pp. 139–61.

23   John S. Saul, *The State and Revolution in Eastern Africa* (London, 1979), pp. 10–11.

24   John S. Saul, 'Mozambique: The New Phase', *Monthly Review*, 30, 10 (1979), p. 15.

25   Marina Ottaway, 'The Theory and Practice of Marxism–Leninism in Mozambique and Ethiopia', in David E. Albright (ed.), *Communism in Africa* (Bloomington, 1980), p. 125.

26   Carole Collins, 'Mozambique: Dynamizing the People', *Issue*, 8, 1 (1978), pp. 12–16.

27   David and Marina Ottaway, *Afrocommunism* (New York, 1981), p. 82.

28   ibid.

29   Saul, 'Mozambique', op. cit., pp. 15–16.

30   D. and M. Ottaway, op. cit., p. 83. For details on these elections, see Allen Isaacman, *A Luta Continua: Creating a New Society in Mozambique* (Binghampton, 1978), Chap. 2.

31   D. and M. Ottaway, op. cit., p. 83.

32   Quotations from Oscar Marleyn, David Wield and Richard Williams, 'Notes on the Political and Organizational Offensive in Mozambique and its Relationship to Agricultural Policy', *Review of African Political Economy*, No. 24 (1982), pp. 119, 120.

33   D. and M. Ottaway, op. cit. p. 207.

34 The following discussion owes much to the argument contained in Jackson and Rosberg, op. cit. pp. 270–86.
35 Billy J. Dudley, *An Introduction to Nigerian Government and Politics* (London, 1982), pp. 130–1, 136.
36 President Houphouët-Boigny of the Ivory Coast at the seventh congress of the PDCI in 1980, quoted in Colin Legum (ed.), *Africa Contemporary Record. Survey and Documents 1980–81* (New York, 1981), p. B515.

6 | African International Relations

We have so much to ask for and so little to bargain with.
Sylvanus Olympio quoted in Vernon McKay (ed.),
African Diplomacy (London, 1966).

In most African countries, the advent of independence was accompanied by a smooth transfer of power. Only a few countries experienced serious internal problems and these were to lead to international repercussions. Belgian withdrawal from the Congo (now Zaire) and Portuguese withdrawal from Angola were followed by intra-state violence and foreign (non-African) intervention. The advent of independence in some other African countries (Djibouti and Spanish Sahara) resulted in a deterioration of relations among African states and inter-African clashes. The withdrawal of Spain from the Sahara, for example, provoked armed hostilities involving Morocco, Algeria and Mauritania. From 1965 Southern Rhodesia represented a further type of international crisis, when white settlers declared UDI (Unilateral Declaration of Independence). Operating from bases in neighbouring countries such as Mozambique and Zambia, Zimbabwean nationalists waged extensive military operations against the white-settler regime whilst the OAU – a grouping of independent African states – and non-African powers (such as Britain and the United States) sought reconciliation through negotiation. These are therefore all examples of Africa's internal crises, consequent upon the attainment of independence, being externalized; and in all of them resolution entailed the intervention, directly or not, of outsiders, whether African or not.

But if independence has at times been followed by international conflict, the goal of majority rule itself has also been (and remains) a major issue with international consequences. The political goal of independence for Namibia is currently an international problem and the question of majority rule in South Africa is also a subject that is increasingly arousing the attention of the world community. African states have sought to end South African rule in Namibia as well as to end *apartheid* and racial discrimination in South Africa itself through diplomatic means, preferably with the support of the United Nations.

127

They have advocated peaceful change and evinced no strong desire to achieve their objectives through force, either through joint African military operations or through the use of foreign (especially Cuban) troops. The Lusaka Manifesto on southern Africa states: 'We would prefer to negotiate rather than destroy, to talk rather than kill. We do not advocate violence . . .'[1] But African states have also recognized that violence and armed struggle are likely. At its inception in 1963, the OAU set up an African Liberation Committee to serve as a channel for financial and military assistance to 'freedom fighters'. Yet there has not been much support for the Liberation Committee by most African countries, or active participation in the armed struggle to liberate territories from white rule. In the cases of the erstwhile Portuguese colonies and Rhodesia, for example, African states and the OAU remained on the sidelines so far as the actual conduct of the liberation war was concerned. To be sure the support, facilities and encouragement of neighbouring countries (as, for instance, Tanzania in the case of Mozambique and Mozambique and Zambia in the case of Zimbabwe) were crucial to the liberation movements in the successful conduct of their many years of armed struggle. Nevertheless, African states have primarily pursued a policy of peaceful negotiation in seeking an end to white rule in southern Africa.

In regard to the diplomatic strategy, African states have sought primarily to persuade the western nations to disengage from South Africa, employing both moral reasoning and, at times, threats of economic action against western economic interests within various independent African countries. They have been successful in having South Africa removed from a number of international organizations although not yet membership of the United Nations; but they have not achieved much in persuading western states to reduce or sever their economic links. Moreover, African countries in the past have been relegated to the sidelines as far as influencing the political outcome of independence struggles was concerned. The OAU was collectively humiliated by its repeated powerlessness to influence events in the Rhodesian crisis. It proved unable to unite the rival nationalist organizations or acquire sole control of their external assistance with which it hoped to further their integration. Mayall writes that 'the failure of the OAU to achieve these two objectives had seriously undermined its capacity to control great power influence in continental affairs'.[2] And, similarly, African states and the OAU have hardly had much impact on developments towards political independence in Namibia. To be sure African states are involved in negotiations over Namibia, but it is the western nations that are determining political outcomes.

That the political leverage African countries have been able to bring to bear on the independence struggles in southern Africa (as well as in other independence crises) has been so minimal is the product of independent

Africa's lack of military means and its strong dependence on western economic interests. In 1965, for example, the OAU called on member states to break off diplomatic relations if Britain failed to end the UDI regime. Only nine out of 40 states implemented this decision. Nor were the African Commonwealth states able to act in concert and sever diplomatic relations with Britain, or disrupt the Commonwealth by leaving it in order to exert pressure. Although some contemplated such drastic action, the 'disruption of the pattern of economic relations that such a withdrawal would have entailed was obviously a serious deterrent'.[3] Similarly, African countries, particularly the Francophone ones, have rarely cut their links with France despite the latter's repeated violation of United Nations' sanctions against arms sales to South Africa. Moreover, the OAU's conciliatory approach to independence struggles (in the ex-Portuguese colonies, Rhodesia and Namibia) not only reflect Africa's military and political weakness but, above all, its abject economic dependence on the West. In addition, it is even more galling to note that although Africa's leaders have fulminated against South Africa at international forums this has not prevented them from agreeing to trade with it. Consequent upon their economic weakness, many if not most African countries have trading links with South Africa. In 1980 South Africa sold sold $1.3 billion worth of goods and services to 40 African countries, whereas ten years earlier South African exports to the rest of Africa had been only $300 million.

It is a truism to state that African countries are weak and dependent.[4] Most of Africa's states are poor, and some are very poor. Two-thirds of the three dozen poorest countries in the world are to be found in sub-Saharan Africa. Africa's economic dependence on the West, the result of colonialism, has already been noted; but this economic dependence has been deepened and extended not least because Africa's economic plight has worsened in the past decade.[5] At least fifteen African countries require foreign budgetary support (usually in the form of grants) to balance their annual recurrent costs; and most of Africa looks to the West for financial support to underwrite its development plans. The food dependency of Africa has also increased greatly in recent years; food aid is required in large quantities by many of its countries. Africa's worsening economic situation has resulted in external debts swelling enormously, the creditors being western commercial banks and financial consortia. The roughly two score nations south of the Sahara account for about an eighth of the Third World's total debt: 'in 1980 the total foreign debt of sub-Saharan governments and public agencies stood at nearly $56 000m out of a total of $450 000 for all developing countries taken together'.[6] More and more African countries, including those such as the Ivory Coast and Kenya, which had achieved high rates of growth in the 1960s and 1970s, have incurred huge foreign debts and have had to resort to the multilateral institutions of the western capitalist system for assistance. There has been a major acceleration in the activity of the International Monetary Fund (IMF) in Africa in the 1980s and World Bank loans have also increased. The hold of foreign capital has grown as well: the expanding role of multinational corporations is to be seen everywhere. A marked multilateralization of western interests has occurred – new trade, aid projects, investment flows, loans – with various countries including ex-colonial ones as well as those such as the United States participating.

The major source of dependence in Africa is still Europe. A form of 'special relationship' has evolved between the Francophone African states and France, in the shape of very close economic, cultural and military ties. French technical assistance is particularly important and around 200 000 French nationals work in Africa under aid programmes. In 1983 some 10 000 French troops and military advisors were maintained in several African countries. The ties between Britain and the Anglophone African countries have not been as close or on a similar scale but there has been important economic, technical and military co-operation. The role that the European Economic Community is playing in Africa is also growing under the auspices of the Lomé Convention. Secondly, the role of the United States and the International Monetary Fund have become important. The involvement of the United States in the continent began to expand in the 1970s. Agreements were concluded giving it the use of military facilities (such as in Kenya) and it has increased its military assistance and arms sales to the region. Its economic links have also developed substantially. Africa's resort to credits from the IMF have made the region a major client of the institution. By the end of 1983, 23 African countries had agreements with the IMF and in view of Africa's mounting debt burden, IMF loans were of central importance.

These various connections as well as Africa's abject weakness and demeaning dependency on western assistance have enabled outside forces to play a prominent role in the continent's contemporary affairs. Military intervention has occurred particularly where western interests (primarily economic ones) have been involved. As early as 1964 western intervention occurred when Belgian paratroopers – transported in American aircraft from a British-held island – made a landing in the Congo to rescue European hostages. The weakness of the OAU in preventing this external intervention was dramatically demonstrated.[7] France has also undertaken military operations to maintain protégés in power (as in Gabon on behalf of President M'Ba in 1964, Zaire in 1977 and 1978, and Chad between 1968–72 and between 1975–80) as well as in the removal of discredited leaders such as Bokassa in the Central African Republic in 1979. All of France's major interventions in the 1970s were in areas where control of raw materials was at stake.[8]

British military intervention has been more limited, having occurred mainly in the early post-colonial years, such as in 1964 when the British government responded to an appeal for assistance from Kenya, Tanganyika and Uganda to put down the army mutinies in East Africa. In 1982, however, the British Special Air Services (SAS) was involved in putting down a coup in the ex-British colony of the Gambia.

More covert forms of intervention in Africa's internal affairs – through economic and diplomatic means and through the operation of western intelligence networks – have, however, been much more common than the use of military force. French investment and assistance programmes have been used to influence domestic politics; and the World Bank attempted during the mid-1970s to exert pressure on Tanzania to abandon her *ujamaa* policy in return for further aid.[9] Covert action by the United States' Central Intelligence Agency (CIA) has been particularly evident in Zaire and Angola – countries with important American interests. CIA covert operations played an essential role in the coming to power of American-approved leadership in Zaire in the 1960s. The United States, concluded one writer, was 'the arbiter of Zaire's political destiny'.[10] Although not directly involved militarily, the United States was also active in destabilizing the Marxist MPLA regime in Angola with Zairean and South African assistance in the mid-1970s in order to attempt to keep Angola within the western sphere of influence in Africa.[11]

The former colonial powers and their ally, the United States, have intervened almost at will in African countries to secure their interests. The inability of African governments to prevent such interventions – consequent upon their lack of military means and economic weakness – has demonstrated clearly their limited influence and control over events in the continent. This inability has been further demonstrated by the growing involvement of Communist states in Africa's affairs.

Up to the mid-1970s, the links that Communist powers had with sub-Saharan Africa were very limited. Aside from diplomatic ties and arms transfers to liberation movements (especially in southern Africa), their connections were essentially low-key. Since 1974, however, the political landscape of Africa south of the Sahara has changed dramatically in that Communist states, and particularly the Soviet Union, have become much more prominent than in the immediate post-colonial years. Together with Cuban combat units, the Soviet Union was deeply involved in the crisis in Angola in 1975–6; it supplied over $300m in military equipment and logistical support. The Soviet–Cuban backing was crucial to the triumph of the MPLA in Angola. In 1984 over 30 000 Cuban military personnel were estimated to be present in Africa and the Communist powers were particularly important in the provision of military aid to a number of the self-avowed Marxist states (such as Ethiopia, Angola and Mozambique). As in the case of the western powers, Soviet military (and the more limited economic) assistance to Africa has been dictated by political relationships, strategic considerations and resource needs. African dependence on such assistance has made the few African countries receiving it increasingly beholden to Soviet interests.[12]

To challenge their external dependency, the main problem to be confronted by African states has been their vulnerability to external control. The small size, population and markets of most African countries, their reliance on earnings from one or two export items, and their dependence on the export sector to finance their development plans, has had to be recognized and resisted. Kwame Nkrumah of Ghana was one of the earliest to suggest political unification – 'a major political union of Africa' – as a means of resisting the problems of 'balkanization' of Africa into small and non-viable states. He further advocated economic co-operation on a continental scale.[13] But amongst Africa's independent political leaders Nkrumah was in a minority of one. Even the OAU, which was formed in 1963 to provide the new African states the protection of a continental institution, seeks to promote only unity and not political unification. The OAU 'is an organization of sovereign states which have agreed to co-operate for certain purposes, but certainly not to create any supra-national authority above themselves'.[14] Actual mergers of African states have rarely occurred; Tanganyika joined Zanzibar in 1964 to form a united republic (the name Tanzania was officially adopted in 1965), while Senegalese and Gambian leaders created a Sene–Gambian confederation in 1982. The OAU did, however, set up an Economic and Social Commission as one of its specialized agencies to co-ordinate economic co-operation, but this has not achieved much. At various summit conferences the OAU has adopted resolutions encouraging African countries to promote inter-African co-operation in economic fields, but the results have been exceedingly meagre. Attempts at economic co-operation at the sub-regional level have also occurred. The continent has witnessed the rise and fall of many regional groupings. Such attempts have proceeded from different concepts and have achieved various degrees of success; but the trend in most of them has been towards disintegration or stagnation.[15]

If the OAU's role in economic matters has been slight, it has been primarily a political institution. The OAU Charter laid down three major areas of activity. Two of these – the promotion of economic co-operation and the liberation of territories still under colonial domination – have been considered briefly above and are further the subject of our southern Africa case-studies below. In both of these aims the OAU has not been too successful. The final aim has been the resolution of disputes among member-states. In this regard as well the OAU has had mixed fortunes. Various types of conflict have tested sorely the OAU's capability for crisis management: border differences, trans-border armed subversion, civil wars and foreign intervention. Numerous disputes have been mediated and resolved, though usually through the good offices of the heads of individual states rather than through the OAU as a collective body.[16] But there have also been disputes where the OAU has either been unable to enforce its decisions (lacking as it does the authority to enforce sanctions or disciplinary measures and being obliged to rely on persuasion and moral force), or where the organization itself has been too internally divided to arrive at a collective decision. Indeed, on Africa's major post-colonial issues such as the Congo crisis (early 1960s), Nigerian civil war (1967–70), Angola (1975–6), and the Western Sahara (1970s and 1980s), the OAU has lacked unanimity, been chronically weak, and of 'very limited use'. Austin further states that it 'was the UN which helped to restore order in the Congo. It was Britain and the Soviet Union which helped the Nigerian federal government to end the civil war'.[17] And the examples could be multiplied. In 1982 the OAU was so divided that it failed twice to muster a sufficient quorum to hold its nineteenth annual summit meeting. The validity of the OAU, in fact, has always been somewhat exaggerated, and its unity is very frail. African member-states have been divided along various lines – ideological, racial (Arab/African) – and have, with the possible exception of southern African independence, rarely been able to agree on important issues. The divergences among African states have not been conducive to the resolution of Africa's various political disputes let alone to inter-state dialogue for unity; nor have they been conducive to lessening the extent of foreign interference in Africa's affairs.[18]

Growing inter-state inequalities may also be significant in the future for continental unity. A small number of 'middle powers' in Africa have advanced their international status (through economic potential and military strength) and achieved a degree of political dominance at the regional level. For instance, the Economic Community of West African States (ECOWAS), which groups together all sixteen countries of the region, is dominated by Nigeria (which accounts for a third of ECOWAS's total budget, 60 per cent of its trade and two-thirds of GNP). The upward movement of a few states such as Nigeria (and Kenya in eastern Africa) is to be contrasted with the majority of African countries which are relatively poor and subordinate. Although such dominance has not led to much political conflict as yet there could be repercussions for African international relations as some states grow progressively stronger and others relatively weaker.

During the 1960s, political disputes among member-states of the OAU rarely involved outbreaks of armed violence. Violence was limited by the modest military capabilities of African states, and by a reluctance to become involved in international conflicts which could prove costly. But during the 1970s, defence expenditure rose appreciably (Leys estimates a fourfold increase between 1965–77 for 28 sub-Saharan African countries, excluding South Africa).[19] The increasing availability of the means to prosecute war has been accompanied by an increasing incidence of intra-African conflict and military intervention.[20] Increasing recourse to force in Africa's conflicts is evident in the violent interventions in Chad as well as in the invasion of Uganda by the Tanzanian army in 1979. (The latter armed intervention, and the maintenance of Tanzanian forces in Uganda until a semblance of order was restored in that country, cost $500m and has had a crippling effect on Tanzania's economy.) On a more limited scale, individual states have intervened to contain armed conflict and to restore order in a neighbouring state. In 1971 Guinean troops came to the assistance of the faltering regime of Siaka Stevens in Sierra Leone. A recent instance, in 1980, was the intervention of Senegalese troops in the Gambia (at the request of the briefly ousted President Jawara) to put down a rebellion and a coup.

The OAU has been able to do little to prevent such interventions, although it has considered, but been unable to create, a permanent military force of its own which could be used in disputes among member-states. The OAU has, however, set up peacekeeping forces which intervened, for example, in the civil war in Chad in 1980 and 1981. The withdrawal of these troops after a few months of expensive inaction demonstrated the limited ability of the pan-African organization to solve Africa's problems. The OAU has remained a useful forum for discussion and negotiation within the continent but it has not had much success in resolving the numerous disputes amongst its members or in building up a consensus among them or in lessening the extent of foreign leverage within Africa's affairs.

Although the foreign policy of African states has been concerned with external themes such as regional integration and liberation of colonial territories, it has also, in large measure, been intimately associated with domestic political requirements.[21] Clapham has written that the 'most basic foreign policy issue confronting the new governments concerned the identity of the state itself'.[22] The preservation of the territorial integrity of the state has been a vital matter. Given the artificial nature of colonially determined boundaries and the fact that many African states are ethnically heterogeneous, not a few have been faced with secessionist claims. Chad, Kenya, Nigeria, Uganda and Zaire are well-known examples. To counter secessionist claims and the threat of dismemberment, support has been solicited from foreign states. Thus, in seeking to contain the threat of Biafran secession and maintain the unity of Nigeria, the government was led, during the years 1967–70, to call on the support of the international system. Nigeria attempted to secure OAU validation for her position vis-à-vis the claims put forward by Biafra to ensure that Biafra was not given recognition as an independent state by other African countries.[23] Other states, notably the Francophone ones, have through their military agreements with the former colonial power been able to counter threats to their integrity. Chad, for example, has on various occasions called upon French military assistance against rebels in the northern part of the country.[24]

African governments have also employed foreign policy to secure their (often precarious) hold on power. 'There are few African regimes which do not regard their foreign policy as integral to their own survival, and opposition to that policy, correspondingly, as treasonable.'[25] In their quest to acquire domestic support, political leaders have, at times, taken actions which have had repercussions on foreign policy. The repudiation of foreign debts (as in the case of Acheampong in Ghana in the 1970s) or the expulsion of non-Africans (as in the case of those living under Amin in Uganda in the 1970s) are two instances of leaders attempting to enhance their internal political positions by popular actions in the external sphere. The possibility of increasing domestic authority through activities in the foreign policy sphere (such as high-level talks and the hosting of international conferences) is another example. President Kaunda's numerous forays in the international politics of southern Africa have been undertaken, in part, to build up his domestic position in Zambia by portraying him as a major international figure. A third example is Dr Banda's policy of co-operation with the white south (particularly the close economic and diplomatic relations with South Africa), which is closely connected with domestic politics. Shortly after Malawi's independence in 1964, a group of cabinet ministers, favouring more radical domestic and foreign policies, broke with Banda. The political crisis that followed influenced Banda's choice of foreign-policy options. Banda's foreign policy has been linked with his reliance on expatriate (including South African) civil servants and security officials to bolster his regime internally and his dependence on South African aid to build a new capital in Lilongwe (the area of his greatest political support). Foreign connections have thus been resorted to in order to assist Banda to stay in power as well as enhance his domestic position.

International politics of southern Africa

The conflict in southern Africa between, on the one hand, the racist system of white-settler colonialism and, on the other hand, the black nationalist liberation movements has assumed major international dimensions. No conflict has united black Africa more than the conflict in southern Africa. The overthrow of colonialism and white racial domination has been a key goal uniting member countries of the OAU and the pan-African organization has been deeply committed to ending white minority rule. The main African countries involved in the liberation struggle are the 'white' south's black regional neighbours – the so-called

Front-Line States. At the same time southern Africa has become intimately connected with super-power rivalry between the USA and the USSR as well as with the East–West cleavage in world politics.[26]

The white minority regimes have attempted to link their struggle to preserve white power and privilege with their self-conceived role as the last 'bastion against Communism'. The fact that the black liberation movements wage an armed struggle and that they receive the bulk of their military supplies from the Soviet Union and other Communist countries has lent credence to the claim of the white-controlled states that they are also engaged in an 'anti-Communist crusade'. The liberation movements are presented as a major component of the world Communist movement, aiming to attain world hegemony and Communist control in Africa. Arguing along these lines, the settler regimes have hoped to strengthen their ties with the West, and in particular the USA, to thwart the influence of the Soviet Union in southern Africa and thereby to maintain white power and dominance in the sub-continent.

South Africa has constituted the stronghold of the 'white' south and has been the dominant power in southern Africa. During the 1960s and early 1970s, in order to achieve its interests of white supremacy, South Africa sought to maintain a ring of white states along its northern borders, which would provide a buffer against the black liberation movements. For over a decade the white regimes of South Africa, Portugal and Rhodesia devised concerted policies to hold the line along the Zambesi. But with the collapse of her Portuguese ally in 1974, South Africa lost the protective shield that Angola and Mozambique had provided. The prospect of political independence being achieved in Rhodesia as well as in South African-occupied Namibia (the former South-West Africa, which South Africa administers illegally in defiance of the United Nations) also began to appear a possibility in the imminent future. Political independence, South Africa began to recognize, could not be forever averted. But the pace and character of political evolution could be influenced, and determined efforts undertaken to promote the coming to power of moderate indigenous governments not supportive of liberation within South Africa itself. In the mid-1970s South Africa came to accept the need to replace the white-settler regime in Rhodesia and worked to have a moderate black government installed to power. In the independence elections of 1980, for example, South Africa provided financial support to the conservative ANC under Muzorewa. Similarly in Angola the South Africans backed UNITA in 1975 and hoped that the Marxist-oriented MPLA would be excluded from power. In Namibia, too, South Africa has worked to build up client groupings which would lead to the establishment of a co-operative, indeed pliable, indigenous government that would exclude the radical liberation movement SWAPO from participation.

South Africa's prime concern is survival, in particular to establish a *'cordon sanitaire'* along its northern borders by replacing the former white buffer with a stable ring of black buffer states. In regard to its black regional neighbours South Africa has followed a stick-and-carrot policy, employing its considerable economic and military preponderance over the black African states. During the 1970s it pursued an economic offensive in regard to its neighbours to the north. In particular, South Africa hoped that trade and aid would lead to the neutralization of the African countries as well as earn her international respectability. Trade and co-operation agreements were entered into with Malawi, while Botswana, Lesotho and Swaziland have remained tied to the South African economy. The 1970s also saw South Africa launch its diplomatic offensive – known as *détente* – towards the region's black-ruled states, promising changes in its domestic policies in order to open a 'dialogue' with black Africa. Diplomatic relations were started with Malawi and high-level missions visited various countries, including the Ivory Coast, Kenya, Zaire and Zambia. These offensives were geared to South Africa's desire to surround itself with a ring of buffer states whose co-operation would be bought with economic assistance in return for their agreement to refrain from interfering in the internal affairs of the Republic. South Africa, however, has only been partly successful in its aims. Most states in the region, although closely tied economically to South Africa, have continued to give material and political support to the liberation movements.

Recent years have seen the militarization of South Africa's policy towards its black neighbours becoming more pronounced.[27] This is the consequence, in part, of the failure of its *détente* policy to achieve much impact; but it is also due to mounting nationalist attacks within South Africa itself. Military raids and bombings of neighbouring countries have occurred ostensibly to weaken liberation movements based there, but they also aim to exert pressure on these countries to withdraw permission for such bases to continue in existence. Thus South African troops have invaded Angola several times to attack the Angolan bases of the SWAPO insurgents into Namibia; and they have also attacked ANC camps in Mozambique and Lesotho to curb operations of the liberation movement into South Africa itself. Complementing direct military attacks has been the policy of destabilization, entailing the provision of military training and equipment to anti-government groups – such as the MRM in Mozambique and UNITA in Angola – to undermine ruling groups. Official Angolan figures in late 1983 reported that South African aggression had cost the country $10 billion and had made over 100 000 people homeless; and guerilla activities seriously dislocated the Mozambican economy. South Africa's military policy appears to have begun to pay dividends. Prime Minister Mugabe repeatedly stated that the South African liberation movements would not be permitted to establish military bases in Zimbabwe as this would only 'provoke South Africa to destroy us'. The beleagured regimes of Angola and Mozambique were forced into talks with South Africa in early 1984; the latter entered into a formal non-aggression and security pact with South Africa, whereby ANC military bases would be dismantled in return for South Africa halting its support of anti-government guerilla movements.

These developments reflect a return to the policy of negotiation. The turn away from the politics of the big stick to those of discussion is also congruent with domestic pressures on the South African government. An influential body of opinion among exporters in South Africa has viewed the MRM as harmful to South African trade. 'The private sector does not want our neighbours to be destabilized', says a senior official in a major export promotion organization, 'because it hurts our markets. The more viable their economies, the better the market potential'.[28] South Africa's regional policies are also closely associated with domestic political pressures.

East–West rivalry has, since 1975, become an increasingly important factor in southern Africa. In that year the Soviet Union and Cuba intervened in Angola to help maintain the MPLA in power. With the USA and other western governments providing military assistance to the anti-government FNLA and UNITA, and the South Africans invading Angola, the Soviets and Cubans responded by sending troops and military supplies which decisively tilted the balance in favour of the MPLA. By the beginning of 1976 some 12 000 Cuban soldiers were in Angola and the Soviets had sent in over $300m of military equipment. In December 1975 the US Senate refused to provide aid for further activities and the South Africans, bitterly disappointed by this refusal, were forced to withdraw. The Cubans have remained, providing a protective presence for the MPLA regime of up to 25 000 soldiers.

The Soviet–Cuban intervention marked a political watershed for the West in the region. Up to 1975, southern Africa had been primarily in the western sphere of influence; and western policy generally had been one of 'benign neglect' towards the region. This was now dramatically altered, especially with the independence in 1975 of Angola and Mozambique, both of which had strong political ties (and, in the case of Angola, strong military connections) with the Soviet Union and eastern bloc countries. The reaction of the West, and particularly that of the USA, was to reassert itself in the affairs of the region, as seen in Secretary of State Dr Kissinger's two safaris to the area in 1976 and the various American diplomatic initiatives since then in seeking resolutions to the conflicts in Rhodesian and Namibia.[29]

With important economic interests at stake as well as strategic and mineral resource considerations, western countries have desired to contain the apparent threat of Communist influence in southern Africa.[30]

From the mid-1970s the western powers came increasingly to realize that their economic and strategic interests in the region, and especially those in Rhodesia and Namibia, could not be long secured by white minority regimes.[31] Acceptance in principle of majority rule and independence in Rhodesia and Namibia, however, was linked with the desire to promote moderate non-radical organizations to state power which would create a stable environment for western investments and keep the Communist threat at bay. The USA, in particular, wanted to establish moderate governments in Rhodesia and Namibia which together with Zambia, Zaire, Malawi, Botswana, Lesotho and Swaziland would form an anti-communist block in the region. Emphasis was consequently placed on independence being attained through negotiation and peaceful solutions rather than through armed struggle. (Kissinger recognized that wars of national liberation could turn nationalist organizations into ideologically radical bodies and, because of their military support from Communist countries, spread the influence of Communist powers in southern Africa.) In addition, promises were made of western economic development assistance for responsible African governments after independence.[32] Ian Smith, the prime minister of the settler regime in Rhodesia, summed up western policy in 1976 in regard to American constitutional proposals: 'Dr Kissinger assured me that we share a common aim and a common purpose, namely to keep Rhodesia in the free world, and to keep it free from Communist penetration.'[33] In Namibia as well the so-called Western Contact Group (those western powers sitting on the United Nations Security Council – the United States, Great Britain, Canada, West Germany, and France) want to prevent a radicalization of the liberation movement SWAPO. Fearful of the further influence the Soviet Union might acquire in the region through its military support for SWAPO, they sought to attain a negotiated outcome and a peaceful transfer of power which would also avoid the Communist intervention that would supposedly ensue if independence was achieved through a war of liberation. Furthermore, the USA refused to recognize the MPLA government in Angola, mainly on account of the large numbers of Cuban troops stationed there. The Americans wanted to end the Cuban and Soviet presence in Angola. To achieve this they linked the independence of Namibia with the withdrawal of Cuban troops from Angola. But the USA also considered removal of Angola's Marxist-oriented rulers. The CIA was involved in covert operations in neighbouring Zaire directed at effecting a change of regime. The West, too, appears to have granted tacit approval to the military actions of the South African army in southern Angola, which seriously disrupted the country's economy and heightened the position of anti-government political organizations.[34] To ameliorate Soviet influence the USA reportedly offered a massive dollar credit for oil development and the EEC considered a major aid programme for Angola.

Developments in Rhodesia, Namibia and Angola have been of inherent importance to the West but they are the prologue to the ultimate issue in southern Africa – that of South Africa. The western and especially American stance in regard to South Africa has been to prod the white regime to make gradual changes on a reformist path to internal transformation. Under its policy of 'constructive engagement' with South Africa,[35] the Reagan administration in the USA urged the bringing together of moderate elements of black and white communities in a mutually advantageous coalition, thus promoting a multiracial political evolution which could be significant in checking African armed resistance as well as promoting local allies favourable to the interests of the West. To be sure the West has repeatedly condemned racialism and stressed that South Africa should moderate her *apartheid* policies; but it has not been outright in its condemnation of continued white minority rule in South Africa. Nor has the West gone beyond polite and mild requests to compel South Africa to end its colonial occupation of Namibia. Indeed, the West is seen by many as the mainstay – economically, politically, and militarily – of South Africa as well as the preserver of white power and the opponent of black liberation. But the partnership is a conflicting as well as complementary one. A community of economic, security and anti-Communist interests binds South Africa and the West. Yet there are tensions and differences that make for a troubled relationship, the consequence, in part, of the West's growing interests in black Africa. The West cannot forever ride the black and white horses at once; and it is this realization that has led it to begin its agonizing reappraisal of support for the racist system in South Africa.[36]

The Soviet Union's infiltration into southern Africa is in line with its determination, as a global super-power, to alter the strategic balance of power between itself and the USA by bringing as much of the third world under its own influence and control (as well as in its desire, within the context of Sino–Soviet rivalry, to counter Chinese involvement in the liberation struggles). Employing its considerable and burgeoning military resources, the Soviet Union and the eastern bloc states are engaged in active military interference in various parts of Africa. In southern Africa it is through the provision of military assistance in national liberation struggles or in its 'fraternal assistance' to countries such as Angola and Mozambique (entailing primarily military aid) that the Soviet Union has attempted to improve its strategic position vis-à-vis the USA in the region. Predominantly through military assistance the Soviets are attempting to expand and consolidate their own geopolitical and strategic positions. But other than in Angola and Mozambique, and in its links with the liberation movements ANC and SWAPO, the Soviet Union has little influence elsewhere in the sub-continent. During the Zimbabwean liberation struggle, for instance, it provided little or no military assistance to ZANU–PF (and the ZANLA guerillas) and has not much support within the new independent government. Moreover, southern Africa is not a central concern in Soviet global strategy and the Soviets would not be too willing to become involved in an East–West confrontation in the region to expand their geopolitical position. What the Soviets seem to be engaged in at the moment is a policy of consolidation (especially in Angola) with a view to expanding their influence at a later stage, should an opportunity arise which was unlikely to lead to major East-West conflict.

The OAU has devoted considerable attention to the problems of southern Africa.[37] Colonialism, *apartheid*, and racial discrimination have been regularly at the top of its agenda since its founding in 1963. OAU policy towards the 'white' south has been a combination of economic sanctions and military force. Economic boycotts and sanctions have, as we have already noted above, not been implemented by most African states; and the strategy of armed struggle has also not been strongly supported. The OAU committed itself in 1963 to a policy of total support for armed confrontation and set up the African Liberation Committee (ALC). But the majority of OAU member-states have not given much financial or material backing to the ALC; and the strategy of armed confrontation has itself been questioned on several occasions.

Although the OAU has supported a double strategy of peaceful negotiation and armed struggle, it has generally preferred the former. On the Rhodesian issue, for example, it gave constant support to achieving a negotiated settlement. By stressing peaceful change the OAU states have demonstrated that Africa operates under major constraints of military weakness that determine its capacity to bring about desired political changes in southern Africa. But such a policy also reflects an ideological commitment to a nationalist solution to the problems of the region. With the exception of a few countries, the majority of African states have been concerned about the potential radicalization of liberation movements and the emergence of Marxist-oriented regimes in the sub-continent.

In 1970 the OAU adopted the Lusaka Manifesto of 1969 (which advocated peaceful negotiation if that would advance the process of decolonization). The importance of the Manifesto lies in its clear enunciation of the opposition of African states to seeing the conflict in southern Africa as part of the ideological struggle between East and West. The people of southern Africa are not 'interested in Communism or Capitalism; they are interested in their freedom. They are demanding an acceptance of the principles of independence on the basis of majority rule.'[38] The preference of the OAU has been for 'positive neutralism' and non-alignment; and the pan-African body has been alarmed by the spectre of an East–West confrontation in southern Africa. Nevertheless, East–West rivalry has intruded into regional problems and had an important bearing on developments there. In part, this is the result of the

OAU urging member-states to use their good offices individually to exercise pressure, especially on western powers to induce political changes. In part, this is the result of external aid solicited in support of the liberation movements. Substantial military and economic assistance has been received from various countries, in particular from the Communist countries. The OAU has attempted to maximize the effectiveness of such assistance to the liberation struggle and to minimize the possibility of big-power intervention in it by insisting that all aid be channelled exclusively through the ALC. The Soviet Union and other Communist states, however, have delivered the larger part of their aid directly to specific liberation movements that they favoured.

These contradictions confronting the OAU are mirrored among the Front-Line States (FLS) (Angola, Botswana, Mozambique, Tanzania, Zambia, and since 1980 Zimbabwe).[39] Since 1976 the OAU has virtually left the Rhodesian and Namibian issues to the FLS. This informal delegation of authority was due, in large part, to the dissension within the OAU itself, chiefly along ideological lines. The FLS have been the main material and political supporters of the liberation movements. The development of armed struggle has been greatly assisted by sanctuaries, supply channels and arms conduits in neighbouring Front-Line States. Yet the FLS have also supported a negotiated settlement over Rhodesia and Namibia and have been willing to accept western proposals provided they guaranteed majority rule. This dual strategy created tensions and differences within the FLS, particularly during the period of the liberation struggle in Zimbabwe. While Mozambique and Tanzania supported armed confrontation, Zambia was concerned about radical governments coming to power in neighbouring Angola and Zimbabwe. Zambia, in particular, maintained secret exchanges with South Africa on the prospects for regional rapprochement and President Kaunda met personally with the South African prime minister. In pursuance of its policy of achieving a peaceful resolution of the Rhodesian dispute, it repeatedly pressured Zimbabwean nationalists to negotiate with the white settlers; it also tended to lend its backing to the more moderate nationalist leaders. In 1975 it even gave encouragement (as did Zaire) to the South African government to intervene against the MPLA in Angola.[40]

The FLS have been able to exercise considerable control over the activities of the nationalist guerilla groups operating against white-ruled territories. But the FLS have been obliged to seek some measure of accommodation with the white minority regimes. The requirements of economic survival have meant that they have had to maintain economic relations with the white south. This contradictory response to the liberation struggle has at times resulted in the FLS coming into conflict with the needs of the guerilla movements. Various examples could be cited. A recent one derives from the serious economic and social disruption in Angola and Mozambique which has forced the governments of these countries to look to South Africa for economic assistance in return for which they have agreed to curb SWAPO and ANC cross-border attacks on Namibia and South Africa from their territories.

By lending their backing to the liberation movements, the FLS have exposed themselves to the military retaliation of the white regimes. They have turned for military aid and material assistance to the East and West. Military and economic dependence on the major powers has rendered the FLS susceptible to foreign pressure to which they have responded in contradictory ways; they seek outside help yet strive simultaneously to avoid being linked too closely with either super-power. Mozambique, for example, has begun to look for military and economic assistance from the West to avoid too close a dependence on the Soviet Union. Zambia, on the other hand, has expanding security and military ties with the Soviet Union to counter-balance its virtual economic dependence on the West. The FLS have wanted to preserve some degree of independence and avoid coming under the exclusive domination of a particular super-power. But it is because Africa does not possess the economic and military might to end white rule in the continent that it has been obliged to seek foreign assistance. This has meant, and will continue to mean, super-power and foreign intervention in the affairs of southern Africa.

Regional co-operation in southern Africa

The Southern African Development Coordination Conference (SADCC) was launched in 1979.[41] Since then nine independent countries (Angola, Botswana, Lesotho, Malawi, Mozambique, Swaziland, Tanzania, Zambia, and Zimbabwe) have come together to promote economic co-operation among themselves. The origin of SADCC can be traced to the alliance of the Front-Line States of Angola, Botswana, Mozambique, Tanzania and Zambia, which had been formed in 1974 and had co-operated in rendering diplomatic and material support to the liberation movements, particularly in Zimbabwe. Now they were coming together to strive towards their own economic liberation. 'The initiative towards economic liberation has flowed from our experience of joint action for political liberation.'[42]

The first objective that SADCC has espoused is 'the reduction of dependence, particularly, but not only, on the Republic of South Africa'. The economic supremacy of the *apartheid* regime in the southern African region is well-known, as is the strong dependent link between most of the nine black states and South Africa. At the launching of SADCC it was stated: 'Southern Africa is dependent on South Africa as a focus of transport and communication, as an exporter of goods and services and as an importer of goods and cheap labour ... Southern Africa is fragmented, grossly exploited by South Africa and is subject to economic manipulation by outsiders.'[43] SADCC therefore declared that the 'dignity and welfare of the peoples of Southern Africa demand economic liberation and we will struggle towards that goal'.[44] South Africa itself has for long urged greater regional co-operation. In order to maintain its economic hegemony (and consolidate its *apartheid* regime) it has, since the late 1960s, proposed various schemes for closer economic relations with its northern neighbours. The latest of these proposals, which also appeared in 1979, is the 'Constellation of Southern African States', which is 'a scheme to bring independent states under the same political economic and military domination by the apartheid regime as the Bantustans'.[45] But none of the independent states has been attracted; instead, they have resolved to overcome or reduce the pattern of dependence on South Africa by maximizing their joint markets and resources to the benefit of their 50 million people through their own regional co-ordination.

Three other objectives have been put forward by SADCC: 'the forging of links to create a genuine and equitable regional integration'; 'the mobilization of resources to promote the implementation of national, interstate and regional policies'; and 'concerted action to secure international co-operation within the framework of our strategy for economic liberation'.[46] With these objectives in the background, the SADCC states have set out certain strategies and priorities. The key to their strategy lies in the field of transport and communications. The plan for economic liberation involves setting up transport and communications links independently of South Africa: 'Without the establishment of an adequate regional transport and communication system, other areas of co-operation become impractical.'[47] Thus although other areas of possible co-ordination, such as food and agriculture, manpower and industry, have been identified, SADCC's first emphasis is on the implementation of transport and communication projects over the next decade.

The creation and future success of SADCC poses a clear challenge to the economy of South Africa. South Africa's response has been immediate. The *apartheid* regime has in various ways stepped up its policy of 'destabilization' in the region. The South African-backed Mozambique National Resistance Movement and UNITA in Angola have attacked strategic targets, thereby disrupting transport and communication links (and possibly strengthening the dependence of these countries on southern routes). South Africa has also embarked on punitive economic measures against the fledgling state of Zimbabwe and there have been various provocations against Botswana, Lesotho and Zambia. Through these and other measures South Africa is seeking to prevent closer unity and to force the majority-ruled states of southern Africa to abandon their independent foreign policy positions involving criticism of *apartheid* and rejection of South African expansionism and hegemony. But the SADCC states are not unaware: a major theme of the SADCC summit meeting of July 1983 was that of South African destabilization which was clearly seen as seeking to keep South Africa's neighbours economic prisoners.

SADCC's preoccupation with South Africa has not been accompanied by much concern to reduce dependence on the advanced capitalist western states.[48] Little has been said about external dependence (foreign investment, transfer of technology) with the latter. Ownership and control of the productive elements of the national economies within SADCC are, however, largely in the hands of foreign capital. *Laissez-faire* integration schemes can result in an increase in dependence, as the large multinational companies in the region reap most of the benefits of integration at the expense of existing or potential indigenous enterprises. That such a possibility exists may be deduced from the alacrity with which foreign capital and international development agencies greeted the formation of SADCC. Indeed, external agencies played an important role in its creation. The United States Agency for International Development (USAID) has from 1978 conducted studies for United States co-operation with the independent countries of southern Africa both individually and on a multi-state or regional basis. The European Economic Community (EEC) too has advocated such regional co-operation and is said to have been the moving spirit behind the birth of SADCC. Moreover, the strategy for economic liberation requires large sums of money to be operational, funds not to be found locally. External financial support is needed; and large sums have been pledged by countries (Italy, USA) and institutions (EEC) from the West to implement the programmes.

The prospects for successful regional co-operation will also depend on the extent to which SADCC can overcome the problems which led to the failure of other integrative schemes in Africa, such as the East African Community. Ravenhill has identified several causes of regional break-down in Africa: first, African economies are characteristically competitive rather than complementary to one another; secondly, the institutional structures created in support of regional arrangements are inadequate and have limited authority; thirdly, gains are not distributed equally between the participating states; and lastly, there are serious ideological differences between the African states.[49]

The SADCC states are fully aware of such problems. Some of them have been members of earlier integrative schemes which proved unsuccessful. Tanzania, for instance, continually complained of the unequal distribution of gains when it was one of the participating states in the East African Community. When the Tanzania–Mozambique Permanent Commission of Co-operation was established in 1976, Tanzania sought to ensure that the benefits would be distributed relatively equally. 'The Permanent Commission, therefore, set up production complementarity as a priority.'[50] SADCC has adopted a similar approach. It entails each country being responsible for a specific sector of activity. For example, Mozambique is responsible for transport and communication, Zimbabwe for agriculture, and Malawi for fish and forestry. The distribution of areas among participating states may be more conducive to resolving problems such as the equitable spread of benefits. Certainly the idea of a common market or a customs union appears to have received little support, being seen as laying the basis for unbalanced development. Such trading arrangements have tended to foster growth primarily in the economically most advanced countries at the expense of the rest and have therefore been avoided; hence the voluntary basis of co-operation implied by the term 'Co-ordination Conference'. The approach adopted may also prevent the creation of elaborate bureaucratic structures by encouraging the decentralization of decision-making processes and the implementation of projects. The problem at the moment, however, is that some countries are not executing their tasks adequately in the specific fields for which they are responsible and also that the central institutional structures lack the authority to ensure that action is taken. Finally, the political heterogeneity of the SADCC group has not so far led to friction; but ideological differences in the various ruling groups as well as their lack of unanimity regarding South Africa could have a crucial bearing on the prospects for successful regional integration.

NOTES

1 *Manifesto on Southern Africa* (Lusaka, 1969), Section 12.
2 James Mayall, 'The OAU and the African Crisis', *Optima*, 27, 2 (1977), p. 88.
3 Yashpal Tandon, 'The Organization of African Unity as an Instrument and Forum of Protest', in Robert I. Rotberg and Ali A. Mazrui (eds.), *Protest and Power in Black Africa* (New York, 1970), p. 1171.
4 For a discussion of this dependence, see Timothy M. Shaw and M. Catharine Newbury, 'Dependence or Interdependence: Africa in the Global Political Economy', in Mark W. Delancey (ed.), *Aspects of International Relations in Africa* (Bloomington, 1979), pp. 39–89.
5 Most African countries are in very serious macro-economic trouble. This is the result of various factors, including governmental inefficiency, corruption and mismanagement as well as difficult external circumstances. For a discussion of the gravity of Africa's economic situation, see World Bank, *Accelerated Development in Sub-Saharan Africa: an Agenda for Action* (Washington, 1981). See also Colin Leys, 'African Economic Development in Theory and Practice', *Daedalus*, 111, 2 (1982), pp. 99–124.

6   Melvyn Westlake, 'Black Africa. The Burden of Debt Continues', *The Times* (London), 1 November 1982, p. 16.
7   See Tandon, op. cit., pp. 1155–64.
8   Robin Luckham, 'French Militarism in Africa', *Review of African Political Economy*, No. 24 (1982), pp. 55–84.
9   *The Guardian* (Manchester), 3 July 1975. See also Cheryl Payer, 'Tanzania and the World Bank', DERAP Working Paper, A285, (Bergen, 1982).
10 See Stephen Weissman, 'The CIA and US Policy in Zaire and Angola', in René Lemarchand (ed.), *American Policy in Southern Africa: The Stakes and the Stance* (Washington, 1978), p. 396.
11 See, for example, Gerald J. Bender, 'Kissinger in Angola: Anatomy of a Failure', in Lemarchand, op. cit., pp. 65–143.
12 See Thomas H. Henriksen (ed.), *Communist Powers and Sub-Saharan Africa* (Stanford, 1981), for a discussion from the viewpoint of American writers. Covert elements of Soviet foreign policy in Africa have also been fairly important: the KGB has supported attempts to overthrow established governments.
13 Kwame Nkrumah, *Africa Must Unite* (London, 1963).
14 Mayall, op. cit., pp. 83–4.
15 See, for example, Abdul Aziz Jalloh, 'Recent Trends in Regional Integration in Africa', *Nigerian Journal of International Affairs*, 6, 1/2 (1980), pp. 71–81.
16 See B. David Meyers, 'Intraregional Conflict Management by the Organization of African Unity', *International Organisation*, 28, 3 (1974), pp. 345–73.
17 Dennis Austin, 'Ex Africa Semper Eadem?' in Roger Morgan (ed.), *The Study of International Affairs* (London, 1972), p. 160.
18 For the tenuousness of African unity, see Zdenek Cervenka, *The Unfinished Quest for Unity: Africa and the OAU* (London, 1977).
19 Leys, op. cit., p. 106.
20 See S. N. MacFarlane, 'Intervention and security in Africa', *International Affairs*, 60, 1 (1983/4), pp. 53–73.
21 See I. William Zartman, 'National Interest and Ideology', in Vernon McKay (ed.), *African Diplomacy. Studies in the Determinants of Foreign Policy* (London, 1966), pp. 25–54.
22 Christopher Clapham, 'Sub-Saharan Africa', in Christopher Clapham (ed.), *Foreign Policy Making in Developing States. A Comparative Approach* (Farnborough, 1977), p. 80.
23 See John J. Stremlau, *The International Politics of the Nigerian Civil War 1967–1970* (Princeton, 1977).
24 See, for example, E. G. H. Joffe, 'The International Consequences of the Civil War in Chad', *Review of African Political Economy*, No. 25 (1982), pp. 91–104.
25 Clapham, op. cit., p. 84.
26 For more extensive discussions of interactions in southern Africa, see *inter alia*, Kenneth W. Grundy, *Confrontation and Accommodation in Southern Africa. The Limits of Independence* (Berkeley, 1973); Colin Legum, 'International Rivalries in the Southern African Conflict', in Gwendolen M. Carter and Patrick O'Meara (eds.), *Southern Africa. The Continuing Crisis* (London, 1979), pp. 3–17; Timothy M. Shaw, 'International Organisations

and the Politics of Southern Africa: Towards Regional Integration or Liberation?', *Journal of Southern African Studies*, 3, 1 (1976), pp. 1–19; John Seiler (ed.), *Southern Africa Since the Portuguese Coup* (Boulder, 1980); Gwendolen M. Carter and Patrick O'Meara (eds.), *International Politics in Southern Africa* (Bloomington, 1982); and Christian P. Potholm and Richard Dale (eds.), *Southern Africa in Perspective. Essays in Regional Politics* (New York, 1972).

27   See Christopher Coker, 'South Africa: A New Military Role in Southern Africa 1969–82', *Survival*, 25, 2 (1983), pp. 59–67.

28   Quoted in John Kane-Berman, 'South Africa's regional strategy', in *Africa Guide 1983* (London, 1983), p. 43.

29   For discussions of US policy towards southern Africa, see the essays in Lemarchand, op. cit.

30   Besides gem diamonds and gold, South Africa is the world's largest producer of chrome, manganese, vanadium, and other minerals. Uranium production in Namibia and South Africa is also increasing. The economic importance of South Africa to the West is further reflected in substantial investments there by over two thousand western companies. And the geographical position of South Africa at the confluence of the Atlantic and Indian Oceans as well as the so-called 'Cape route' have given South Africa some strategic importance. The West, for example, wishes to secure passage for the bulk of its tankers carrying oil from the Persian Gulf around the Cape to western Europe.

31   This was at variance with the previous US policy of supporting white regimes in southern Africa. See for example *The Kissinger Study on Southern Africa* (Nottingham, 1975), introduction by Barry Cohen and Mohamed A. El-Khawas.

32   See David Martin and Phyllis Johnson, *The Struggle for Zimbabwe: The Chimurenga War* (London, 1981), pp. 235–6, 255.

33   Quoted in ibid., p. 254.

34   See Michael Wolfers and Jane Bergerol, *Angola in the Frontline* (London, 1983), Chap. 11.

35   See Christopher Coker, 'The United States and South Africa: Can Constructive Engagement Succeed?', *Millennium Journal of International Studies*, 11, 3 (1982), pp. 223–41.

36   See, for example, Hedley Bull, 'The West and South Africa', *Daedalus*, 111, 2 (1982), pp. 255–70.

37   See Cervenka, op. cit., Chap. 8 on 'OAU Policy and Strategy in Southern Africa'.

38   Manifesto, op. cit., Section 14.

39   For an introductory discussion of the Front Line States, see Robert S. Jaster, *A Regional Security Role for Africa's Front-Line States: Experience and Prospects*, Adelphi Papers, No. 180 (London, 1983).

40   See Martin and Johnson, op. cit., Chap. 8 and pp. 232–3.

41   For a more detailed discussion, see Arne Tostensen, *Dependence and Collective Self-Reliance in Southern Africa. The Case of the Southern African Development Coordination Conference (SADCC)* (Uppsala, 1982). See also Douglas G. Anglin, 'Economic Liberation and Regional Cooperation in

Southern Africa: SADCC and PTA', *International Organisation*, 37, 4 (1983), pp. 681–711.

42   SADCC, *Southern Africa: Towards Economic Liberation*. Declaration by the Governments of Independent States of Southern Africa made in Lusaka, 1980.

43   SADCC, *Towards Economic Liberation*. Declaration by the Front-Line States made in Arusha, 1979.

44   SADCC (Lusaka, 1980), op. cit.

45   Journalist quoted in Carol Thompson, 'Front Line Focus', *Southern Africa*, 14, 3 (1981), p. 31.

46   SADCC (Lusaka, 1980), op. cit.

47   ibid.

48   See Anglin, op. cit., pp. 696–700 for a discussion of these external linkages.

49   John Ravenhill, 'Regional Integration and Development in Africa: Lessons from the East African Community', *Journal of Commonwealth and Comparative Politics*, 17, 3 (1979), pp. 227–46. See also *The African Review*, 8, 1/2 (1978) for an entire issue devoted to a discussion of the disintegration of the East African Community.

50   Carol B. Thompson, 'Regional Strategies of Development: From the Frontline States to SADCC', *Ufahamu*, 11, 3 (1982), pp. 61–6.

Select
Bibliography

The following is a selected list of the more important books and articles on contemporary African politics. It is related to the various topics considered in this book.

General

Allen, C. and Williams, G. (eds.), *The Sociology of 'Developing Societies'. Sub-Saharan Africa* (London, 1982).
Cohen, D. L. and Daniel, J. (eds.), *Political Economy of Africa. Selected Readings* (London, 1981).
Europa Publications, Ltd., *Africa South of the Sahara* (London, annual).

1 Towards Political Independence

Austin, D., *Politics in Ghana, 1946–1960* (London, 1964).
Bates, R. H., *Essays on the Political Economy of Rural Africa* (Cambridge, 1983), Chap. 4.
Cliffe, L. R., 'Nationalism and the Reaction to Enforced Agricultural Change in Tanganyika during the Colonial Period', *Taamuli*, 1, 1 (1970), pp. 3–15.
Coleman, J. S., 'Nationalism in Tropical Africa', *American Political Science Review*, 48 (1954), pp. 404–26.
Coleman, J. S., *Nigeria: Background to Nationalism* (Berkeley and Los Angeles, 1958).
Coleman, J. S. and Rosberg, C. G. (eds.), *Political Parties and National Integration in Tropical Africa* (Berkeley, 1966).
Epstein, A. L., *Politics in an Urban African Community* (Manchester, 1958).
Hodgkin, T., *Nationalism in Colonial Africa* (London, 1956).
Iliffe, J., *A Modern History of Tanganyika* (Cambridge, 1979).
Joseph, R. A., *Radical Nationalism in Cameroun. Social Origins of the UPC Rebellion* (Oxford, 1977).
McCracken, J., *Politics and Christianity in Malawi, 1875–1940* (Cambridge, 1977).

150

Maguire, G. A., *Toward 'Uhuru' in Tanzania. The Politics of Participation* (Cambridge, 1969).

Morgenthau, R. S., *Political Parties in French-Speaking West Africa* (Oxford, 1964).

Odinga, O., *Not Yet Uhuru* (London, 1967).

Onselen, C. van, *Chibaro: African Mine Labour in Southern Rhodesia 1900–1933* (London, 1976).

Phimister, I. R. and Onselen, C. van, *Studies in the History of African Mine Labour in Colonial Zimbabwe* (Gwelo, 1978).

Rathbone, R., 'Businessmen in Politics: Party Struggle in Ghana, 1949–57', *Journal of Development Studies*, 9, 3 (1973), pp. 391–401.

Wasserman, G., *Politics of Decolonization. Kenya Europeans and the Land Issue 1960–1965* (Cambridge, 1976).

2 Conflict, Coalitions and Coups

Barrows, W. L., *Grassroots Politics in an African State: Integration and Development in Sierra Leone* (New York, 1976).

Cohen, M., *Urban Policy and Political Conflict in Africa. A Study of the Ivory Coast* (Chicago, 1974).

Cox, T. S., *Civil–Military Relations in Sierra Leone. A Case Study of African Soldiers in Politics* (Cambridge, Mass., 1976).

Decalo, S., *Coups and Army Rule in Africa. Studies in Military Style* (New Haven, 1976).

Dunn, J., (ed.) *West African States. Failure and Promise* (Cambridge, 1978).

Molteno, R., 'Cleavage and Conflict in Zambian Politics: a Study in Sectionalism', in W. Tordoff (ed.), *Politics in Zambia* (Manchester, 1974), pp. 62–106.

O'Brien, D. B. Cruise, *Saints and Politicians. Essays in the Organization of a Senegalese Peasant Society* (Cambridge, 1975).

Sandbrook, R., 'Patrons, Clients, and Factions: New Dimensions of Conflict Analysis in Africa', *Canadian Journal of Political Science* 5, 1 (1972), pp. 104–19.

Sklar, R., 'Political Science and National Integration – A Radical Approach', *Journal of Modern African Studies*, 5, 1 (1967), pp. 1–11.

Wolpe, H., *Urban Politics in Nigeria. A Study of Port Harcourt* (Berkeley, 1974).

3 State and Economy

Arrighi, G. and Saul, J. S., *Essays on the Political Economy of Africa* (New York, 1973).

Beckman, B., 'Whose State? State and Capitalist Development in Northern Nigeria, *Review of African Political Economy*, No. 23 (1982), pp. 37–51.

Collins, P., 'Public Policy and the Development of Indigenous Capitalism: The Nigerian Experience', *Journal of Commonwealth and Comparative Politics*, 15, 2 (1977), pp. 127–50.

Ergas, Z., 'The State and Economic Deterioration: The Tanzanian Case', *Journal of Commonwealth and Comparative Politics*, 20, 3 (1982), pp. 286–308.

Eriksen, K., 'Zambia: Class Formation and Detente', *Review of African Political Economy*, No. 9 (1978), pp. 4–26.

Leys, C., *Underdevelopment in Kenya. The Political Economy of Neo-Colonialism* (London, 1975).

Leys, C., 'African Economic Development in Theory and Practice', *Daedalus*, 111, 2 (1982), pp. 99–124.

Mwansasu, B. U. and Pratt, C. (eds.), *Towards Socialism in Tanzania* (Dar es Salaam, 1979).

Ottaway, D. and M., *Afrocommunism* (New York, 1981).

Rosberg, C. G. and Callaghy, T. M., (eds.), *Socialism in Sub-Saharan Africa. A New Assessment* (Berkeley, 1979).

Saul, J. S., *The State and Revolution in Eastern Africa* (London, 1979).

Swainson, N., *The Development of Corporate Capitalism in Kenya 1918–77* (London, 1980).

Young, C., *Ideology and Development in Africa* (New Haven, 1982).

4   *Classes and Politics*

Amey, A. B. and Leonard, D. K., 'Public Policy, Class and Inequality in Kenya and Tanzania', *Africa Today*, 26, 4 (1979), pp. 3–41.

Baylies, C. L. and Szeftel, M., 'The Rise of a Zambian Capitalist Class in the 1970s', *Journal of Southern African Studies*, 8, 2 (1982), pp. 187–213.

Beer, C. E. F. and Williams, G., 'The Politics of the Ibadan Peasantry', *The African Review*, 5, 3 (1975), pp. 235–56.

Cohen, R., 'Class in Africa: Analytical Problems and Perspectives', in R. Miliband and J. Saville (eds.), *The Socialist Register 1972* (London, 1972), pp. 231–55.

Diamond, L., 'Class, Ethnicity, and the Democratic State: Nigeria, 1950–1966', *Comparative Studies in Society and History*, 25, 3 (1983), pp. 457–89.

Jeffries, R., *Class, Power and Ideology in Ghana: The Railwaymen of Sekondi-Takoradi* (Cambridge, 1978).

Sandbrook, R. and Cohen, R. (eds.), *The Development of an African Working Class: Studies in Class Formation and Action* (London, 1975).

Schatzberg, M. G., *Politics and Class in Zaire. Bureaucracy, Business and Beer in Lisala* (New York, 1980).

5   Political Control, Participation and Institutionalization

Callaghy, T. M., 'State–Subject Communication in Zaire: Domination and the Concept of Domain Consensus', *Journal of Modern African Studies*, 18, 3 (1980), pp. 469–92.

Cliffe, L. and Saul, J. (eds.), *Socialism in Tanzania*, 2 vols. (Dar es Salaam, 1972–3).

Collier, R. B., *Regimes in Tropical Africa, Changing Forms of Supremacy, 1945–1975* (Berkeley, 1982).

Jackson, R. H. and Rosberg, C. G., *Personal Rule in Black Africa. Prince, Autocrat, Prophet, Tyrant* (Berkeley, 1982).

Kasfir, N., 'Departicipation and Political Development in Black African Politics', *Studies in Comparative International Development*, 9, 3 (1974), pp. 3–25.

Mamdani, M., *Imperialism and Fascism in Uganda* (London, 1983).

Tordoff, W. (ed.), *Administration in Zambia* (Manchester, 1980).

Young, C., 'Zaire: The Unending Crisis', *Foreign Affairs*, 57, 1 (1978), pp. 169–85.

6   African International Relations

Anglin, D. G., 'Economic Liberation and Regional Cooperation in Southern Africa: SADCC and PTA', *International Organization*, 37, 4 (1983), pp. 681–711.

Carter, G. M. and O'Meara, P. (eds.), *International Politics in Southern Africa* (Bloomington, 1982).

Cervenka, Z., *The Unfinished Quest for Unity: Africa and the OAU* (London, 1977).

Chaliand, G., *The Struggle for Africa. Conflict of the Great Powers* (London, 1982).

Clapham, C., 'Sub-Saharan Africa', in C. Clapham (ed.), *Foreign Policy Making in Developing States. A Comparative Approach* (Farnborough, 1977), pp. 75–109.

Henriksen, T. H. (ed.), *Communist Powers and Sub-Saharan Africa* (Stanford, 1981).

Lemarchand, R. (ed.), *American Policy in Southern Africa: The Stakes and the Stance* (Washington, 1978).

Ravenhill, J., 'Regional Integration and Development in Africa: Lessons from the East African Community', *Journal of Commonwealth and Comparative Politics*, 17, 3 (1979), pp. 227–46.

Index